31 Prayers for Spiritual Wealth

A Biblically Based Prayer Strategy for Small Business Owners

Chanel E Martin

DEDICATION

I dedicate this book to my children Cydney and Cue, may you forever
be spiritual wealthy.

CONTENTS

CONTENTS

ACKNOWLEDGMENTS

I'd like to acknowledge everyone who participated in the inaugural Blessed Profits 31 Day Business Prayer Challenge. Your participation, support, and prayers helped me to write this book. Thank you for letting me pray for you.

INTRODUCTION

For our struggle is not against flesh and blood, but against the rulers, against the authorities, against the powers of this dark world and against the spiritual forces of evil in the heavenly realms. [Ephesians 6:12 NIV]

I remember when I first learned how to pray. My grandmother Julia Rogers sat me on my knees next to her bed and taught me The Lord's Prayer.

Our Father which art in heaven, Hallowed be thy name. Thy kingdom come, Thy will be done in earth, as it is in heaven. Give us this day our daily bread. And forgive us our debts, as we forgive our debtors. And lead us not into temptation, but deliver us from evil: For thine is the kingdom, and the power, and the glory, for ever. Amen. [Matthew 6:9-13 KJV]

The Lord's Prayer was my first introduction to prayer, and every night before I would go to bed, we would get on our knees and recite it word for word. My grandmother did her best to explain to me, a small five-year-old child what each line of the prayer meant. The next prayer I committed to memory was the 23rd Psalm.

The Lord is my shepherd; I shall not want. He maketh me to lie down in green pastures: he leadeth me beside the still waters. He restoreth my soul: he leadeth me in the paths of righteousness for his name's sake. Yea, though I walk through the valley of the shadow of death, I will fear no evil: for thou art

1

with me; thy rod and thy staff they comfort me. Thou preparest a table before me in the presence of mine enemies: thou anointest my head with oil; my cup runneth over. Surely goodness and mercy shall follow me all the days of my life: and I will dwell in the house of the Lord for ever. [Psalm 23 KJV]

The Lord's Prayer and the 23rd Psalm were the foundation of my prayer life. I would go on to pray these two prayers every night before bed throughout my adolescent years. I soon realized that praying just The Lord's Prayer and the 23rd Psalm wasn't enough. I began to get more specific in my requests. When I didn't want to get in trouble for being mischievous, or if I didn't study for an exam and was about to take a test, or even if I lost my keys to my car, I would pray. I didn't fully understand how prayer worked, but I was always told that we could ask God for anything, and believe me I did.

The older I got, the more I prayed. I remember when my life took a significant hit. Most of my prayers were centered around getting out of trouble or for things I wanted. In the summer of 2004, I woke up with the most excruciating pain in my legs. My feet began to swell shortly after that, and I could hardly walk. I had never experienced any major health issues and was a scared college sophomore. I was in the doctor's office nearly every week when school started back that fall. In 2005, after much prayer, blood work, and tests, the doctors discovered that I had an autoimmune disease, Rheumatoid Arthritis. At the time, my mom's insurance wouldn't cover me as a student in Atlanta. I remember praying and asking God for help because I needed to see a doctor and to get on medication to help with my condition.

God quickly answered, and I was approved for a two-year study where I got paid for every doctor visit, and all my medications were free. It didn't matter if my mom's insurance covered me or not, I would see the doctor for free! I knew that this was a God-sent miracle. I didn't have to live in pain, stiffness, and suffering anymore. I was so grateful that God heard and answered my prayers – I experienced and finally understood the power of prayer.

In 2012, along with three other young women from Georgia Tech, I cofounded a hair technology company. We had our fair share of wins and losses, and good and bad times. Of course, I prayed and prayed for us to be successful and to become the leading force for black women in technology. God answered my prayers, because in

2013 we won the Technology Association of Georgia Business Launch Competition and would go on to win several other awards and grace the pages of printed and online publications nationwide. On the outside, we looked like we were building a powerhouse brand that set the tone for other female entrepreneurs, but a piece of my soul was dying which each disappointment and failure.

It felt like my prayers were no longer as effective, and while we'd experience a little success, shortly afterward, we'd suffer defeat. My heart, confidence, and spirit were so weary as I didn't understand why my prayers were going unanswered. After experiencing one of the most devastating seasons of my life, God began to speak to me concerning my prayer life.

God wanted to answer my prayers, he wanted me to win, he wanted me to prosper, but I was doing it wrong. I found out that I needed a prayer strategy surrounding every aspect of my life. God started ministering to me on the correct way to get my prayers through to him. For the time of the simple prayers had come to pass, and Satan was doing everything possible to keep me from walking in my divine purpose.

Satan's goal was to fill me up with hurt, bitterness, resentment, and disappointment towards entrepreneurship, even when I knew for a fact that God had called me to be a Kingdom Builder. The enemy attacked me in my finances, my health, my marriage, and my confidence. The Lord introduced a "new to me" concept on praying for my businesses and showed me how the enemy was set out to attack my purpose. God also taught me that Satan attacks Christian entrepreneurs, because when the wealth of the wicked returns to the righteous, we will become a Kingdom solution to the world's problems. Satan was working double-time to make sure that Christian business owners failed.

God downloaded into me everything that I needed to free my family and my businesses, and how to release every blessing, favor, and resources that were assigned to my purpose. I learned that I could live a life of overflow and abundance and I didn't have to be angry or jealous of what God was doing in other people's lives and businesses, I could ask him, and he would provide. I learned that to receive answers to my prayers that I needed to pray the word of God.

You want what you don't have, so you scheme and kill to get it. You are jealous of what others have, but you can't get it, so you fight and wage war to take it away from them. Yet you don't have what you want because you don't ask God for it. [James 4:2 NLT]

Every word of God proves true. He is a shield to all who come to him for protection. [Proverbs 30:5 NLT]

Such things were written in the Scriptures long ago to teach us. And the Scriptures give us hope and encouragement as we wait patiently for God's promises to be fulfilled. [Romans 15:4 NLT]

Shortly after I began praying from the scriptures in the Bible, God healed me from Rheumatoid Arthritis. Next, he healed my husband from depression that he suffered from for nearly twenty years. The Lord sent me prophetic words and prophets to release his word concerning my life and my purpose. We broke generational curses, released inheritances, received healing and restoration, and improved our finances within a few short months of following the prayer strategy presented in this book. No matter how much wealth, fame, or resources you have in the natural realm, if you are not well in the supernatural you will not experience the fullness of the peace and prosperity that God has for you.

For our struggle is not against flesh and blood, but against the rulers, against the authorities, against the powers of this dark world and against the spiritual forces of evil in the heavenly realms. [Ephesians 6:12 NIV]

31 Prayers for Spiritual Wealth is a biblically based prayer strategy for Christian entrepreneurs. This book was designed to heal you, push you, motivate you, and release every blessing that is owed to you. In this book, you will pray the word of God loose breakthroughs in your business and family life.

This book can be read daily like a devotional, and you can use it as a business prayer manual to create customized prayers. For best results, I encourage you to recite each prayer out loud and have each person in leadership connected to your business recite the prayers along with you. Some of these prayers you will need to read multiple times to experience a breakthrough, and others you will experience instant manifestations. The goal is to get you accustomed to praying the word of God over your business. For the Bible says that we are to never stop praying. [1 Thessalonians 5:17 NLT]

Heavenly Father, I love you, honor you, and adore you, for there is none in all the heavens and the earth like you. For you are great, and your name is full of power. [Jeremiah 10:6]

Lord, I repent for all sins I have committed both known and unknown, and I pray that no plan, scheme, or plot from the enemy will prosper against me, my family, and my business. I pray that all that the prayers in this book will heal, deliver, and bless me and my business.

Father, as I say each prayer I will rejoice always, pray continually, give thanks to you in all circumstances; for this is your will for me to belong to Jesus Christ. [1 Thessalonians 5:16-18]

Father, I will have confidence when I approach you, that if I ask anything according to you will, you will hear me. [1 John 5:14]

Lord, when I seek you in prayer, I will believe and not doubt, because the one who doubts is like a wave of the sea, blown and tossed by the wind. [James 1:6]

For I know that through my prayers and your provision of the Spirit of Jesus Christ that I will be healed, delivered and set free [Philippians 1:19].

Lord, hear my prayer, listen to my cry for mercy; in your faithfulness and righteousness come to my relief. [Psalm 143:1] In Jesus name, I pray amen.

PRAYER ONE: FORGIVENESS

But when you are praying, first forgive anyone you are holding a grudge against, so that your Father in heaven will forgive your sins, too. [Mark 11:25 NLT]

I was one of those people who never held a grudge growing up. I would even struggle to stay mad at people and would write myself reminders that I wasn't supposed to talk to "so and so". I remember one day, my mother made me so upset, that I wrote a sticky note "Don't talk to mom" on my bedroom door. As I look back over my life as a teenager; my heart was so pure and ripe.

As I got older, I experienced more hurt, pain, and disappointment. Those experiences were often tied to the decisions that people connected to me had made. I have felt rejected, unloved, hurt, frustrated, abused, and misused at the hands of others. My heart grew colder and colder with each situation, and that little girl who never held a grudge began to disappear. I felt like people needed to be held accountable for what they had done to me. I believed that if I forgave them, then I was letting them get away for mistreating me. My unforgiveness led me to become the judge, jury, and prosecutor for everyone that had wronged me.

When I would think about certain situations or issues that I had with people and even with myself, my chest would ache, and I would experience a shortness of breath. Every time I would experience those symptoms, I would pray and ask God to take it away. I prayed, and I prayed, and the pain would leave me for a short period. As soon as I would see or hear something related to the issues I had, the pain would come back. I had a forgiveness problem, not a pain problem. My unforgiveness had turned into bitterness and was wrecking havoc on my body.

At church, I signed up to become an intercessor and met with our instructor early morning before church service for class. One of the very first topics we learned was how unforgiveness and bitterness would hinder us from adequately praying for others and ourselves. In the class, we were instructed to write a letter to God about anything and everything that has hurt us. We also had to write a letter to people who have wronged us, and to those we had yet to forgive. I had to be honest with how I felt, and I had to allow my heart to forgive because I didn't want anything hindering my prayers from getting answered.

I tell you, you can pray for anything, and if you believe that you've received it, it will be yours. But when you are praying, first forgive anyone you are holding a grudge against, so that your Father in heaven will forgive your sins, too. [Matthew 11:24-25 NLT]

As you begin reading the prayers in this book, I encourage you to open your heart for forgiveness and get rid of any bitterness that might be dwelling in you. Write a letter to God and unload all of the hurt, the pain, anger, and resentment that you have been holding on to in your heart. Identify those who have wronged you and those who you are struggling to forgive. Once you have identified him or her, write a letter of forgiveness to each person. It doesn't matter if that person is dead or alive. And finally, write a letter of forgiveness to yourself. Forgive yourself for every sin you have committed, allow yourself to be set free. You do not have to carry the burden of your sins no matter how great or small. Our Father loves us so much that he sent his son Jesus Christ to free us from all guilt, pain, embarrassment, bitterness, frustration, and disappointment as a result of our sins.

Father God, I submit to your will, honor you, and give you all the glory and praise. I acknowledge that you are my Lord and Savior. I turn to you to repent so that all my sins may be wiped out and request that you refresh my body, mind, and spirit.

[Acts 3:19]

Lord I confess my sins both known and unknown and I know that you, who is faithful and just will purify me from all unrighteousness. [1 John 1:9]

Lord, I also repent for any decisions/actions that may reflect poorly on my business that I may have committed against you including jealousy, comparing myself to others, coveting other business owners, not using proper discernment, over or underpricing, over or undervaluing myself or my work, mistreating my employees/staff, poor customer service, not operating in integrity, misuse or misappropriation of business funds, not reporting proper income to IRS, and (add anything else that isn't listed).

Father, I humble myself, pray, seek your face, and turn from my sinful ways. I ask that you hear my prayer O Lord and forgive me. [2 Chronicles 7:14] For Father, you are forgiving and good and abounding in love to all who call you. [Psalm 86:5]

Lord I also forgive others that may have wronged me in my business including belligerent customers, poor partnerships, and anyone who may have lied, stolen, mistreated me and (add anything else that isn't listed). Father as I pray, I choose to forgive those who have sinned against me so that you Father in heaven, will forgive my sins. [Mark 11:25]

Thank you Lord for your son Jesus Christ which whom the forgiveness of my sins is granted to me. For it is through him and my belief that I am set free from all my sins. [Acts 13:38-39]

Just as Jesus's flesh died on the cross, I will kill my flesh daily to walk in your goodness and mercy and to be led by the Holy Spirit [Galatians 5:24-25] In Jesus name I pray, amen.

PRAYER TWO: FAITH

Now faith is being sure we will get what we hope for. It is being sure of what we cannot see. [Hebrews 11:1 NLT]

When we are kids, we believe that we can do, be, and have anything we could ever want, there were no limits. I was that kid. I had dreams of becoming an entrepreneur and working in the hair and beauty space, becoming an engineer, and an actress. I knew that I could do it all, and no-one could tell me differently. I had so much faith in my ability to accomplish my goals that I have done just about everything that I dreamed of (except becoming an actress). As I reflect on my life, I have crushed almost every single goal that I have set for myself all because I believed that I was the able and good enough.

In 2005 I was diagnosed with Rheumatoid Arthritis (R. A.) while I was a student at Clark Atlanta University in Atlanta, GA. The onset of the illness was frightening because I had never suffered any major illnesses. I will never forget waking up one day in my dorm room with my legs in so much pain and my feet were so swollen that I couldn't even fit in my size eight shoes. I went to the campus nurse weekly to figure out what was going on, until finally, they had a specialist send me to Grady Hospital in Atlanta, GA to give me a diagnosis. I was told that I had an autoimmune disease and I would have it for the rest of my life. I would have to take medication daily for there was no cure.

I was relieved but also devastated when I heard the news, but I accepted that this was something I had to live with forever and I would make the best of it. I experienced flair ups, achy and stiff joints, and pain over the next ten years until one day the Holy Spirit challenge me. I heard him whisper to me "you have prayed for everything else, but you have never asked for your body to be healed." The Holy Spirit was right. I had never asked God to heal me simply because I didn't have faith that I could be healed. The doctors told me that I would live with R.A. for the rest of my life and I believed them. I had heard of God "miraculously" healing others, but I didn't believe it for myself.

I remember hearing my pastor preach that if you pray the living word of God, then God must answer your prayers. I began to research scriptures in the Bible that talked about healing, and I wrote them down in a notebook. Every single day, I'd wake up, and I would recite those verses out loud. Not only did I pray the word of God, but I shifted my faith to believe that I too could be healed. A few weeks later in a dream, God told me to go to a healing meeting hosted by Evangelist Reinhard Bonnke. God said that I would be healed at that meeting and that I would learn how to heal others.

I was obedient, and my family and I canceled our plans for that weekend and attended the meeting. Every single thing God had shown me was true. The next day I found out I was pregnant with my son Cue, and shortly after becoming pregnant my doctors advised me to stop taking my R.A. medicine. Do you know that haven't had to start back taking my medicine to date! God actually healed my body from R.A. just as he said he would. I had to have enough faith to: believe that he could do it, believe that he could do it for me, be obedient with what he instructed me to do, and continue to pray until my healing manifested.

This was my first time experiencing a supernatural healing, little did I know that God was going to use me to heal my husband from depression that he had been battling with since he was a child (I will tell you all more about that later). I want to tell you that God is still in the business of performing miracles for those who have faith. Whatever it is that you are asking God to do for you, your family and your business - your first step to receiving is believing. For faith is confidence in what we hope for and assurance about what we do not see. [Hebrews 11:1]

Father God, I love you, adore you, honor you, worship you, and lift up your holy name. You are a beautiful, and magnificent God that can do all things. For just as you have created the heavens and the earth, you also created me. You are my Father, my provider, my waymaker, my healer, and you love me to no end.

Lord, I repent for any unbelief I may be harboring. I repent for giving up and for believing that you can't perform miracles for even me. I ask that you forgive me for having little faith, and for not coming to you for all things. For your word says that whatever I ask for in prayer, if I believe that I have received it, and it will be mine. [Mark 11:24]

I also repent for only going through the motions when asking for (name anything that applies) for my business. For when I ask, I must believe and not doubt, because the one who doubts is like a wave of the sea, blown and tossed by the wind. [James 1:6]

Father, I pray that out of your glorious riches you may strengthen me with power through your Spirit in my inner being, so that Christ may dwell in my heart through faith. And I pray that I will be rooted and established in love. [Ephesians 3:16-17]

May you, Lord of hope, fill me with all joy and peace as I trust in you, so that I may overflow with hope by the power of the Holy Spirit. [Romans 15:13]

I ask that you remove all unbelief and lack of faith from my heart. I will believe in you even when my faith is tested through trials because I know that the testing of my faith produces perseverance. [James 1:3]

For it is with my heart that I believe and I am justified, and it is with my mouth that I profess my faith and I am saved. [Romans 10:10]

Father, give me the courage and strength to move in obedience in alignment with my faith for, in the same way, faith by itself, if it is not accompanied by action, is dead. [James 2:17] In Jesus name, I pray, amen.

PRAYER THREE: FEAR

*For God has not given us a spirit of fear and timidity, but of power,
love, and self-discipline. [2 Timothy 1:7 NLT]*

Fear keeps you bound, it keeps you from walking in your purpose,
and it is a tool of the enemy that is used to kill your hopes, dreams,
and future. When you are young, or just starting something you new,
you are often fearless. You are willing to risk it all to yield your
desired results, no matter what. You don't care about what people
think; you don't care if no one gets it, you just "do"! Then
somewhere along your journey, fear stepped in and attempted to
abort your mission.

After suffering many disappointments, I went from fearless to
fearful. When I used to approach everything with boldness and
excitement, I would reluctantly do the things I knew I needed to do
for my business. I was afraid of everything, I was afraid of failing, I
was afraid of succeeding, I was afraid of what others thought, I was
afraid of what others didn't think about me. I soon learned how to
work through the fear, but even the simplest tasks were scary and
frustrating. I couldn't operate at the level that God needed me. Fear
is from the enemy, the devil, also known as your adversary. He
doesn't want you to succeed in doing the will of the Lord EVER!

*For in him all things were created: things in heaven and on earth, visible and
invisible, whether thrones or powers or rulers or authorities; all things have
been created through him and for him. [Colossians 1:16 NIV]*

So we know that God created everything except fear according to 2 Timothy 1:7.

For God has not given us a spirit of fear and timidity, but of power, love, and self-discipline. [Timothy 1:7 NLT]

If God, the creator of all things, did not create fear, then the ruler of this world, Satan, must have created it [John 12:31]. God doesn't ever want us to live a life of fear! This includes fear of starting that business, fear of failure, fear of man, fear of dying, fear of being hurt, and the list goes on. I want you to commit to breaking up from fear. Proclaim that fear will never keep you in bondage, and keep you from experiencing the fullness of God.

Think about it, how many times have you given up or not even started because of fear. Many of you are praying for God to work a miracle in your life and your business, but he can't because you are afraid to make the first move. I made a decision that fear would never overtake me and that I would approach everything God has commissioned me to do with boldness.

In whom we have boldness and access with confidence by the faith of him. [Ephesians 3:12 KJV]

Make a list of everything that you fear as it pertains to your business. Next to each listed fear, name ways that you can overcome each fear.

Dear Abba, Father, Holy One. Father God, please help me to identify areas in which I am fearful including ways to overcome each fear. Lord, I release all fears for I know that you are with me. I will no longer be anxious, for you are my God and you will strengthen me, help me, and uphold your righteous right hand. [Isaiah 41:10]

I repent in the name of Jesus for every time fear has stopped me from operating in your will. Including fear of: my business failing, not being good enough, success, growth, expansion, what others think, loss of relationships, the unknown, following your commandments, not having influence, submitting to your

will and (name anything that wasn't listed).

I command the spirit of fear to leave, in the name of Jesus, the spirit of fear does not belong to me. The Lord has given me power, love, and a sound mind to walk in my purpose, His perfect will. [2 Timothy 1:7]

In my business, and in all of my business activities, I will be strong and courageous. I will not be terrified to do the work in which you have called me to do; I will not be discouraged when things don't work out as planned, or by the whispers of the naysayers. I vow to no longer be worried, upset, or afraid. [John 14:27]

Lord, I pray to you and ask that you free me from all of my fears today at this very moment [Psalm 34:4]. I am strong in the Lord and the strength of his might. I put on the full armor of God, and I can stand firm against any and all plots from the enemy. In Jesus name I pray, amen.

PRAYER FOUR: REJECTION

What shall we say about such wonderful things as these? If God is for us, who can ever be against us? [Romans 8:31NLT]

Overcoming rejection can be a hard battle to fight simply because it is often hidden in other issues. For me, the spirit of rejection was hidden in perfectionism, and every single thing I did had to be perfect. I had a hidden fear that people would reject what I was presenting to them if it was not perfect. I would joke about being a perfectionist, and I wore it with a badge of honor. But on the inside, it would torment me and often keep me from moving forward on critical tasks, or it would take me a long time to accomplish simple tasks. I was worried about the smallest details, and when things didn't go as planned, I would freak all the way out.

My husband would gaze at me in wonderment each time I had a meltdown because he always thought everything I did was great. On the flip side, everything I did was done in "excellence," but the stress and strain to get to said "excellence" would completely wear me all the way down. It was hard for me to find inner peace. I needed to understand that "done" and "executed" was better than perfect. I know that I left money and opportunities on the table because of me being a perfectionist.

My spirit of rejection also showed up in my relationships both business and personal. As a business owner, it is YOUR job to sell your products, and if you are worried about if others will accept and approve what you are doing, then there is a chance that entrepreneurship will be hard for you. I had to get over my fear of talking and asking people to buy my products; I had to get over being told NO. I made a conscious decision that my business success was depending on my ability to put myself and my products out there no matter what. This even included if one or one hundred people purchased my products. If I was rejected or told no, then I needed to say to myself that they were not in my target audience. I had to recover quickly and move on to the next.

My experiences with being rejected formed a false identity in my mind that I wasn't good enough unless it was perfect, no one would buy from me unless it was perfect, no one would listen to me unless it was perfect. I searched and searched to reach the point of perfection and would always come up short. This false identity would bleed over to my relationships with my friends and family. I would be extremely defensive and ready to remove people from my life at the first sign of inconsistency, or if I felt as though they were rejecting a part of me. I closed myself off from growing friendships and networking with other like-minded entrepreneurs.

I am so happy that God has completely and totally healed me from the spirit of rejection. He showed me the source of my rejection and gave me the chance to repent and forgive those who have rejected me. I am now able to work faster, more efficiently, and I can walk boldly in my God-given purpose. Have you ever felt rejected by friends, family, and business? If so, I want you to make a list of everything and everyone that has rejected you and give it to God. For the Bible says if God is for us, who can be against us. [Romans 8:31] If God is always on our side, and we are walking in obedience, then no man can ever come against what God has purposed us.

Lord, I love you, I adore you, I lift up your name. Father, I thank you for creating me in your image. [Genesis 1:26] I know that even if my family, friends, father, or mother abandon me, you will always take care of me. [Psalm 27:10]

Lord, I ask that you reveal your love to me. I allow your heavenly love to enter in my heart. Show me how long, how high, and how deep your love is. May I experience the love of Christ, though it is too great to understand fully. Then I will be made complete with all the fullness of life and power that

comes from you. [Ephesians 3:18-19]

Father I have felt rejected by people not loving me the way I thought they should, from things not working out the way I thought they should, from family and friends, and those I hold close to my heart and from (name anything that isn't listed). Lord, I repent for owning the rejection, I also repent for not seeing myself the way you see me despite how others may feel about me. Please reveal and remove any spirit of rejection from my heart.

Lord I know you have called me to (business, project, ministry etc.) And if you have called me to it, no one can take it away - even those who reject me.

Father your word says that your grace is all that I need and your power works best in my weakness. So I lay all my weaknesses at your feet so that your power can work through me. I will take pleasure in my weaknesses, and in the insults, hardships, persecutions, and troubles that I suffer for you Lord, for when I am weak, then I am strong. [2 Corinthians 12:9-10]

Lord, I repent for any negative words and thoughts that I have spoken that take ownership of the rejection I felt. I repent for any negative words and thoughts that I have spoken to or about someone else because of feeling rejected. Please break any all word cures that were spoken and thought in the name of Jesus.

Father, I forgive those who have aided in me feeling rejected including family, friends, associates, and business partners and I ask that you bless them. In Jesus name I pray, amen.

PRAYER FIVE: SUBMISSION

Teach me to do your will for you are my God. May your gracious Spirit lead me forward on a firm footing. [Psalm 143:10 NLT]

I'll admit, I had an issue with submission, coming from a single parent household I saw my mother do it all - she was a one woman show. I inherently picked up that characteristic as a now married woman with children. Because submission wasn't taught or even understood, not only did I have trouble submitting to my husband, but I had trouble submitting to authority (if I didn't agree with them), and most important, issues with submitting to my Heavenly Father. I felt that I was the one that was responsible for me and that I needed to come up with all of the solutions. I struggled with the notion of letting God lead me and submitting to his will. I took to heart the Bible verse: faith without works is dead, when in fact I could've bypassed a lot of pain and heartache if I just would have given it all to God instead of trying to make it happen.

After test after test, and trial after trial, I finally began to understand what it meant to submit. I needed to surrender ALL to him. From a practical standpoint, this included: not worrying about issues, not getting ahead of his timing (waiting for things to work out instead of forcing them), seeking counsel from God before making any moves, and getting out of my own way. Seeking council from God is a concept that hinders most Christians from fully submitting to God's will. It sounds good in theory, but it takes a relationship with him and patience. Most of us are "too busy" to even spend fifteen to thirty minutes out of our day to seek God for guidance. We put everything at the top of our priority except waiting to hear from God on our next move.

No sooner than I committed to surrender and to submit ALL things to God, things began to work out far better than I could have imagined. Learning to submit to my Father, has taught me how to submit to my husband, and leadership - even if I don't agree or like them. It also took the worry and the weight of having to figure out everything. I know now that if I continuously pray about it and leave it at his feet, he will guide me in the right direction. I may not know how or when things will work out, but I know that God's will, will never fail me.

I know we all have a vision for how our business should work, the type of people we want to serve, and what kind of influence we should have. I challenge you to take a moment each day and declare that you will submit to God's will for your business. Spend five to twenty minutes asking him how you should structure your day, what kind of connections you should make, and what key activities you should participate in.

Dear Heavenly Father, I honor you, adore you, love you, and worship you. I am at peace with yielding to your will, and I know that as a result good will come to me. [Job 22:21]

Lord, I repent for trying to do things my own way and not submitting to your will for my life and my business. I also repent for not submitting to those you have put in authority over me including church leaders, bosses, parents and (insert anything that wasn't listed). Lord, I am happy to submit to your will, for your law resides in my heart. [Psalm 40:8]

Father God, teach me how to submit to your will, let the Holy Spirit lead and direct my path. [Psalm 143:10]

I recognize that I can do nothing in my business of my own strength, I will wait for your instruction. I know that your instruction will never leave me astray because I did not seek my own will, but the will of my Heavenly Father. [John 5:30]

Lord, I will not be conformed to desires of this world and my flesh, but transformed by the daily renewing of my mind including seeking you in prayer, attending church service, and reviewing your word, so that I can be a living example of your perfect will. [Romans 12:2]

Father, equip me in every good way to do your will, so that I may be pleasing in your sight through your son Jesus Christ who will receive all the glory. [Hebrews 13:21]

From now on I will only live by the mantra "If it is the will of the Lord, it will be done." [James 4:15] I ask that your will be done on earth for my business as it is in heaven. [Matthew 6:10] In Jesus name, I pray, amen.

PRAYER SIX: OBEDIENCE

Because one person disobeyed God, many became sinners. But because one other person obeyed God, many will be made righteous. [Romans 5:19 NLT]

Obedience is such an interesting topic for most of us struggle with doing what we want to do vs. what we ought to do. I had issues with obedience because I also didn't understand how to submit to the will of God. I wanted to operate out of my fleshly desires and not in what God had instructed me to do. In early 2017 I was going to launch a hair product line. If you know me, or are familiar with my story, then you know that I am a hair enthusiast.

Having started two hair and beauty companies, launching my line of hair products felt like a logical next step. I knew that God had called me to ministry, more specifically to minister to his entrepreneurs, but making hair products was what was easy, and what I loved to do. I ignored my gut feeling in starting Blessed Profits, because, to be honest, I wasn't interested. I didn't feel qualified to speak on behalf of God, and I didn't feel qualified to minister to entrepreneurs. So I did what was safe - as a mastered degreed chemical engineer, I created a whole line of products in less than a week.

Even though creating the products came easy, and I probably could have been successful - I knew that this wasn't the will of God for my life in this season. I began to feel a heavy tug and pull in my spirit, and I was convicted daily. The Lord said something to me one day - he said, if you teach my people about business - then you will never be broke. This was paramount because we were in one of the driest seasons financially that we had ever experienced. My husband was fired from his job a few months earlier, and we had just had a newborn baby.

God continued to send people to pour into me, uplift me, and to build my confidence - he was shaping me to be the woman of God that he called me to be. After much pain and agony from trying to do it my way, I decided to submit to the will of the Lord. Because of my obedience, my family has been blessed. We've encounter miracles, including my husband being completely healed from depression, and we came out of our dry season. I started to see what looks like to be obedient, including stepping away from what was "easy" to carry out the will of God.

I share this story because you might be in a place where God is calling you to be obedient - to do his will, and not what is "easy". Easy doesn't always mean that it is from God! I want you to think long and hard about the thing you are supposed to be doing that you haven't. Maybe you heard God tell you to do it, or you had a dream, or you feel a tugging in your spirit. Whatever it is, you need to do it and be obedient. For the Lord spoke to me and said - your blessing is on the other side of your obedience, and your inheritance is tied to your obedience.

Father, I just want to thank you and lift up your Holy name. I thank you for always being with me, and never leaving me, despite at times, when I am not listening and heading your instructions for my life. I repent for trying to do things my way and not following the specific instructions that you have poured into me. There are things that I know I should be doing, things you have spoken to me in the night hour, dreams that you have given me that you are waiting to manifest. For it is a sin to know what we ought to do and not do it. [James 4:17]

Father I repent for not honoring you by doing (name anything that isn't listed), for I know it is you who has instructed me to do this.

Lord, I know that I show my love to you by keeping your

commandments. [John 14:15]

For Father, you said that if I keep your commandments that I will be your treasured possession. [Exodus 19:5]

Father, I cast down every thought that would cause me to be disobedient to your word and your will for my life as I train my thoughts to be obedient to your will.

Lord, give me patience and endurance to keep your commands and to remain faithful to Jesus. [Revelations 14:12] For many times what is a quick and easy fix is not always what is right.

Father, I thank you in advance for the increase, blessings, favor, and grace that is coming to my business, my life, and my family. For your word says that if I walk in obedience to all that you have commanded me to do, I will live, prosper, and my days will be prolonged in the land that I will possess. [Deuteronomy 5:33] If I fully obey you and carefully follow all of your commands that you give me today, you will set me high above all the nations on earth. [Deuteronomy 28:1]

Father, I will not only listen to what you have told me to do, but I will also do what you have instructed me. [James 1:22] For just as through the disobedience of the one man the many were made sinners, so also through the obedience of the one man the many will be made righteous. [Romans 5:19]

Lord thank you for choosing me and appointing me for this season, so that I will bear lasting fruit, and that everything that I ask in your name, you will grant it to me. [John 15:16] In Jesus name I pray, amen.

PRAYER SEVEN: GRATITUDE

Devote yourselves to prayer with an alert mind and a thankful heart.
[Romans 8:28 NLT]

There are times in your life when your hearts desires do not match your reality. As long as you are living, you will experience difficult seasons, but it is in those difficult periods that your character will be exposed. It is important that through everything you are going through bad or good, difficult or easy, that you practice gratitude.

Gratitude is when you are thankful even when things aren't going the way you planned. Gratitude is being able to praise and thank God for the good and bad. Gratitude is holding on to the vision that God gave you even when everything looks as if it will never manifest. Gratitude is believing that even though your situation seems impossible to fix, you are trusting and knowing that God is going to follow through on his promises to you. Gratitude is sharing your testimony and being transparent about what God has brought you through. Gratitude is a mindset and a matter of your heart.

I've had to practice gratitude at several moments in my life. 2016 and the beginning of 2017 were one of the most challenging time periods for me and my family. We had a dramatic lifestyle change, our finances took a major hit, my husband was diagnosed with depression and lost his job and health insurance, I lost my dad and my Nana days apart, my marriage seemed hopeless, and I experienced some major setbacks in business.

During that time period we received several prophetic words that my husband and I were headed into our best years in our marriage, business, and finances. Although I believed the words that were spoken over my life, I had no idea how they would manifest. Most days felt impossible to get through, and it appeared that instead of heading towards our best years, we were living in our worst years. Every day I'd ask the Lord to give me strength because despite how bad I felt, I had to show up for my two small kids and my husband (who was battling depression at the time).

I began to thank God in advance for his promises, even though I didn't have a clue when or how they would work themselves out. I fasted, prayed, praised, and worshiped God in the midst of my storm. I also began a gratitude challenge with my friend, where every day we would send each other a minimum of three things we were grateful for. As I began to practice gratitude, my life began to transform for the better. Everything that I prayed for, fasted for, and worshiped for, began to manifest before my eyes.

I am a living example that God can turn it around and work everything out in your favor and his will! For the enemy comes to steal, kill and destroy, but the Lord comes so that I may have life, and I may have it more abundantly. [John 10:10] I challenge you to make a list of everything you have prayed for and start thanking God in advance for those things. I also challenge you to make a list of three things you are grateful for over the next week.

Father God I honor you, praise you, and lift up your name. Father, I thank you for giving life, but also abundant life [John 10:10]. I thank you for sending your son Jesus Christ to die on the cross for my sins for you gave me the victory through him. [1 Corinthians 15:57]

Father, I thank you for giving me the vision for my business/ministry/nonprofit. I am thankful even when things don't go as planned, or didn't work out the way I envisioned it; I am still grateful that you chose me to do your will.

Father God, I repent for any resentment, bitterness, anger, frustration, rebellion, and disobedience that I committed as a response to not practicing gratitude. More specifically I repent

for (List anything that isn't listed), although it didn't pan out the way I expected, I know that that in all things you will work for my good for I love you and have been called according to your purpose. [Romans 8:28]

Lord, even when I am having trouble holding on to your promises, I will rejoice always, pray continually, give thanks in all circumstances; for this is your will for me in Christ Jesus. [1 Thessalonians 5:16-18]

Through all things including in my business, my relationships, my finances, my (List anything that isn't listed) I will give thanks to you, Lord, with all my heart and I will share my testimony. [Psalm 9:1]

Let your peace Lord rule in my heart since as members of one body I was called to peace. And be thankful. Let your message dwell among me richly as I teach and admonish one another with all wisdom through psalms, hymns, and songs from the Spirit, singing to God with gratitude in my heart. [Colossians 3:15-16]

I devote myself to prayer, being watchful and thankful. [Colossians 4:2] Thank you, Lord, for you are good and your love endures forever. [1 Chronicles 16:34] In Jesus name I pray, amen.

PRAYER EIGHT: EMOTIONAL STRENGTH

Don't worry about anything; instead, pray about everything. Tell God what you need, and thank him for all he has done. [Philippians 4:6 NLT]

If you stay in business long enough, you are going to go through some emotional strain. The emotional stress can be caused by not closing enough clients this month, not selling enough houses, your products are going through a slow period, or that partnership fell through. You prayed and prayed and prayed that things would work out the way you wanted, but for some reason or another, you were left empty-handed. This happens to all of us, as business owners and Christians we are going to experience tough times. We turn to family, friends, associates, anyone that will listen, and most of the time, if they are not a business owner themselves, they just won't understand. This can lead you to feel isolated, alone, like a failure, frustrated, nervous, and a whole host of other feelings. It can even cause you to question whether or not you heard God to start your business, project, ministry, nonprofit, etc.

Sometimes things don't work out for a variety of reasons, but if you are walking in your divine purpose, living a holy life, submitting to the will of God, everything you need is already working itself out. You just need to call on your Father to give you the strength to endure the process. It is in the process that you receive those heavenly downloads, confidence, courage, and the strength to carry out your earthly assignment. I am not here to say that it's going to be easy because for most of us, including myself it's hard. But God.... But God... But God is with you through the process; he has never left you, he's always there. When you feel weary about tomorrow, when you feel like you can't endure anything else, when you feel like giving up, all you have to do is call on our Father to renew your strength and to give you peace.

Even as I write this, my eyes are filled with tears and joy, as I recall all the moments that I felt like giving up and that God had forgotten me. I am reminded that it was through my pain, my discomfort, my failures that birthed a mighty warrior for Christ. I am so grateful that God kept me through my most difficult times and gave me the strength to keep going, to keep pushing, even when people, circumstances, and my finances wanted me to abort my purpose before she was born. I understand that every tear, that every failure, every uncomfortable season, taught me how to survive and to allow God to move on my behalf.

God says that he loves you, sons and daughters, he says that if you are reading this and are in the process of giving up, he wants you to not rely on your own strength, but to cry out to him - he is working it out for you. You may not understand why you are in this season, why you had to go through this, but soon it will all make sense. Your life is not a ball of confusion, even when you made poor decisions for your business, yourself, and for your family - he is going to use that as part of your story. So don't try to go at this alone, call on his name and allow him to give you the strength, for your weeping is only for a little while, and your joy comes in the morning. If you have not yet experienced a tough season in your business or your life, remember this prayer, for it will be useful when you need it most.

Father God, I honor you and thank you for creating me in your image. Thank you, Lord, for being an everlasting God, the creator of all the earth that never grows weak or weary. [Isaiah 40:28]

I lift up your name oh Heavenly Father. Lord, I thank you for giving me the strength to do all things through you. [Philippians 4:13]

I ask that you give me power and strength where I am weak. Although at times I may become weak, tired, and exhausted, I put my trust in you and know that you will give me a new strength. Help me to soar high on wings like eagles and not grow weary. Allow me to walk and not faint. [Isaiah 40:29-31]

Oh Lord, I am crying out for your help, please restore my mental health. [Psalm 30:2]

Father, I need you to show me that you are still with me, show yourself to me, remind me of your unfailing love.

God, thank you for being my refuge and my strength whenever I need and call on you. I command in Jesus name that the spirit of anxiety come out and I demand that the root spirits of burden, false responsibility, fatigue, weariness, nervousness, restlessness, and heaviness leave in the name of Jesus. I forgive those who may have hurt me emotionally, and I repent for any self-inflicted emotional damage that I may have brought upon myself. Lord, I give you all my worries and concerns for I know that you care for me. [1 Peter 5:7]

Lord send the Holy Spirit to remind me not to worry, but to pray instead and to tell you all that I need, and to thank you for all that you have done. Give me your peace, oh Lord, and guard my heart and mind as I live in your son Christ Jesus. Fix my mind on what is true, honorable, right, pure, lovely, and admirable. Help me to think about things that are excellent and worthy of praise. [Philippians 4:6-8] In Jesus name, I pray, amen.

PRAYER NINE: HEALING

He said to her, "Daughter, your faith has healed you. Go in peace and be freed from your suffering. [Mark 5:34 NIV]

Your health is essential and is often a place the enemy loves to attack. If you are not healthy or well, then it can be difficult for you to accomplish the Lord's work. Most of us are led to believe that getting sick is apart of life and there is nothing we can do about it, but this is far from true. Like I mentioned before, I suffered from Rheumatoid Arthritis and was healed after taking medicine for ten years. My husband suffered from Dysthymia, a form of chronic depression, since he was in middle school and is healed. Together God has healed us from both mental and physical ailments, but our healing came with a lot of faith, obedience, fasting, and prayer.

I always knew something was a little off in my husband since we started dating in 2007. He would experience highs and lows and never was satisfied. It wasn't until we were pregnant with our second child in 2016 that I finally got an answer to my prayers. My husband Chris decided to go to counseling after getting demoted from his job. The therapist confirmed my suspicions, and he was diagnosed with Dysthymia. Chris had lived with it most of his life, and all of our relationship. He was able to go to a few sessions before he got fired from his job due to poor performance, a side effect of the depression.

My husband was the only one working because I took time off from entrepreneurship to take care of our small children. We were an unemployed, uninsured family with a two-year-old and a three week old newborn, and a newly diagnosed depressed father. My life hit an all-time low. We didn't have much money, nor could Chris see a therapist, but I knew that I wasn't all out of options. I would do whatever it took to see my husband through, and I believed that Chris could be healed. Let me explain exactly what we did to bring forth his healing.

First I had faith, I had to fill in the gap for my husband where he lacked faith. Second, we fasted and prayed - I prayed every single day for his healing. I prayed, and prayed, and prayed like I never prayed before. I knew that if God could heal me, he could heal Chris. I would thank God in advance for the healing that was already in progress. Third, we joined and got active in a church. I knew that it was important for us to be covered and connected with Godly people. Fourth, we had other people praying for us too. We both were very open about his battle with depression and solicited friends, family, and our church family to pray for us and to encourage us.

Fifth, we started tithing and giving, even though at times we had little to no money in the bank. We gave God his money first before we did anything. Sixth, we went through deliverance. I asked God to show me in the spirit realm what was happening with my husband. I cast out every demon that was assigned to him and broke generational curses from me and his bloodlines. Seventh, I moved out of the way and let God work in him. I stopped nagging him and fussing at him when he didn't do something right, and I took complete responsibility for our household. Eighth, we created an environment that wouldn't trigger his depression, we were conscious of the food we ate, exercised, and removed ourselves from stressful situations. In July of 2017 during one of our prayer fasts, my husband woke up and told me that he didn't feel depressed anymore, he was healed! The whole process took only a year.

For my family, it was Rheumatoid Arthritis and Depression, for you it may be something else. I am here to tell you that you do not have to live with sickness, pain, or any infirmities. I am not telling you to not go to the doctor and get treatment for your illness; I am saying that you don't have to agree with the report your doctor gives you. When God sent his son Jesus to die on the cross for our sins, we were freed from sickness and disease.

But he was pierced for our rebellion, crushed for our sins. He was beaten so we could be whole. He was whipped so we could be healed. [Isaiah 53:5 NLT]

Father, I thank you for being a healer. Thank you for sending your son Jesus Christ to die on the cross for my sins so that I can be healed. I worship you, adore you, and honor you. There is none like you. I give all the glory to you God, who is able, through your mighty power at work within me, to accomplish infinitely more than I might ask or think. [Ephesians 3:20]

I praise you LORD, my soul, and forget not all your benefits— you who forgives all my sins and heals all my diseases, who redeems my life from the pit and crowns me with love and compassion. [Psalm 103:2-4]

Lord, I repent for any doors I may have opened that became a doorway for sickness and infirmity to enter into my body and mind. I repent from: not taking care of my body, not getting enough rest, for working too hard, for not eating properly, for not believing that I too can be healed, and for (name anything that isn't listed). I ask that you forgive me of all of my sins both known and unknown.

Father God, I am calling you for help, for I know that you will heal me. [Psalm 30:2] I want to be at my best health to walk in my purpose, serve my customers, and to care for my family.

Lord, I am crying out to you to save me from all sickness and distress including (name sickness or disease). Send me your word Father and heal me, rescue me from the grave. Father, I give thanks to you for your unfailing love and your wonderful deeds for mankind. [Psalm 107: 19-21]

I cancel any word curse that I may have spoken that has taken ownership of having (name any negative words you may have spoken). I cancel any report given or spoken by my doctor or person of authority acknowledging that I have (name sickness or disease). For you, Lord has spoken to me and said, "Son or

Daughter, your faith has healed you. Go in peace and be freed from your suffering." [Mark 5:34]

Thank you, Lord, for sustaining me in my sickness and restoring me from all illnesses. [Psalm 41:3] In Jesus name I pray, amen.

PRAYER TEN: WORD CURSES

Understand this, my dear brothers and sisters: You must all be quick to listen, slow to speak, and slow to get angry. [James 1:19 NLT]

Our words are indeed powerful, so powerful that the Bible is full of instructions on how we should choose our words and be conscious of what we speak. Our words have the power to shape how we think about ourselves and others. When we speak life and blessings, we become motivated to accomplish things we could never have imagined.

Wise words satisfy like a good meal; the right words bring satisfaction. The tongue can bring death or life; those who love to talk will reap the consequences. [Proverbs 18:20-21 NLT]

Despite a few setbacks here or there, I can truly admit that I have lived an awesome life! I know for a fact it was due to the love and positivity that was spoken over me as a child. My mother always pushed me to excellence and led me to believe that I could do anything within the will of God. This very small, but powerful act allowed me to pursue opportunities from scholarships, to pageants, to even starting businesses.

I found out later that everyone wasn't privileged to have the supportive upbringing that I had. There were mothers and fathers that would speak so much death and negativity over the children, that they believed that for themselves. Some of those same people would ask me how I got this scholarship, or good grades, or an opportunity, and they thought that you had to be special. I would always respond "Well, I saw an opportunity, and I went after it, I believed that I could achieve it and achieve it in excellence."

From the fruit of their lips people are filled with good things, and the work of their hands brings them a reward. [Proverbs 12:14 NLT]

As I got older, when life got real, I started to lose my "can do" attitude. When disappointment or failure would set in, I began to believe and speak negativity over myself and my business. I was guilty of saying things like, they are never going to pay for this, or this isn't going to work so why try, I will never make the money I want to make, I can't-do this, this is hard, and so on. I bet you can figure out what happened next. Those things happened - I experienced the worst financial setback of my life and nearly lost everything! I killed things before they even had a chance to manifest. Once I changed my thinking and begin to speak positivity, my life dramatically changed for the better.

For, Whoever would love life and see good days must keep their tongue from evil and their lips from deceitful speech. [1 Peter 3:10 NIV]

Father God, I come to you today and lift up your Holy and heavenly name. I thank you for giving me words to communicate and to speak love and blessings over your Kingdom.

Lord, I desire to have conversations full of grace, seasoned with salt, so that I may know how to speak to everyone. [Colossians 4:6]

Father show me how to be quick to listen, slow to speak, and slow to become angry so that words I speak will be productive Godly words. [James 1:19]

Lord I repent for any word curses that were spoken over myself including: I'll never be good enough, no one will buy my products or services, I'll never make my revenue goals, I can't-

do this, this isn't going to work and (List anything that isn't listed). I will speak with wisdom, and faithful instruction is on my tongue. [Proverbs 31:26]

Father I also ask that you forgive word curses that I may have spoken over others and their businesses including: I hope their business fails, nobody wants to buy that, they'll never make it, and (List anything that isn't listed). Lord, we will no longer let any unwholesome talk come out of your mouths, but only what is helpful for building others up according to their needs, that it may benefit those who listen. [Ephesians 4:29]

Lord, I forgive anyone who has spoken word curses against me, and I ask that you bless them and their families. Please undo any word curses that were spoken against me, and I ask that you remove those word curses from your heavenly courts.

Lord, set a guard over my mouth and keep watch over the door of my lips. [Psalm 141:3] for those who guard their mouths and their tongues keep themselves from calamity. [Proverbs 21:23] In Jesus name I pray, amen.

PRAYER ELEVEN: GENERATIONAL CURSES

Christ redeemed us from the curse of the law by becoming a curse for us, for it is written: "Cursed is everyone who is hung on a pole.
[Galatians 3:11 NIV]

You may or may not be familiar with generational curses. I know up until the past year I didn't fully understand exactly what it was. I thought that It was just something your family had that you couldn't shake and you would always be plagued with it. Until the Holy Spirit had me listen to the audiobooks **Operating in the Courts of Heaven**, and **Unlocking Destinies in the Courts of Heaven** by Robert Henderson that I began to understand generational curses and how they prevent God from legally granting an answer to your prayers or releasing your inheritance.

I have personally seen the amazing benefits of breaking generational curses from my bloodline and my husband's bloodline. There were opportunities that I knew I should have gotten and things that I should have been healed and delivered from were not manifesting in the physical realm because of generational curses. Some of you may wonder what an example of a generational curse is. Sometimes these curses are very well known - like the fact that everyone in your family get's diabetes, or if you all struggle with gambling, or if most of the people in your family are living in poverty. Sometimes generational curses are harder to pinpoint - like how your mom, grandma, and great-grandma may have some sort of mental illness, or you might have a secret addiction, and your dad or mom struggled with the same issue.

In the old testament, you see very clearly that God punished whole generations for the sins of their ancestors. (Deuteronomy 5:9). There is good news! For we are redeemed by the blood of Jesus Christ, and we can break free of generational curses through repentance for our sins and the sins of our ancestors as mentioned in Exodus 20:5-6, you can be punished from the sins of your parents, but God can also bless your entire bloodline if you love and obey his commandments.

Take a moment to make a list of common afflictions and sins that may plague your family. Think back to stories that were told to you about your grandparents and great grand parents. Once you have a list of known sins, you need to repent of those sins on behalf of your family using the prayer below.

Father God, we lift up your holy and heavenly name. We honor you, love you, adore you. For you are the King of Kings and the Lord of Lords. We come to you today to ask that you break any generational curses that may have afflicted my father, and my father's father's father including (name known sins and afflictions).

Lord I repent for any all sins that I may have committed both known and unknown. Including sins of lust, perversion, double mindedness, unforgiveness, lying, stealing, bitterness, pride, and (name anything that isn't listed).

Father, we execute the verdict of setting forth by the death of Jesus Christ, and we ask that every transgression, sin, and inequity be washed away with the blood of Jesus Christ. For your son, Christ has redeemed us from the curse of the law by becoming a curse for us. [Galatians 3:13] Father through your son we are set free. [John 8:36]

I pray the prayer of Nehemiah: O Lord, God of heaven, the great and awesome God who keeps his covenant of unfailing love with those who love him and obey his commands, listen to

my prayer! Look down and see me praying night and day for your people Israel. I confess that we have sinned against you. Yes, even my own family and I have sinned! We have sinned terribly by not obeying the commands, decrees, and regulations that you gave us through your servant Moses. [Nehemiah 1:5-6 NLT]

In the name of Jesus, I now renounce and break every curse that was handed to me by my ancestors, and I cast the curse off my life back to hell from whence it came. I also loose my future generations and myself from curses that were passed down to me through my bloodline.

I pray that any and all curses that are preventing me from advancing in business according to your will, will be broken and cast out in the name of Jesus, amen.

PRAYER TWELVE: WORSHIP

Give praise to the Lord, proclaim his name; make known among the nations what he has done. [Psalm 105:1 NIV]

I grew up in a very traditional and typical missionary Baptist church. Every Sunday morning you would get a program from the usher and the order of service hardly ever changed. I was also a member of the children's choir and then the youth choir. We'd sing an A&B selection on fourth Sunday like clockwork. I loved my church, and it was all that I knew, it shaped my beliefs and taught me my foundation that I stand on today. But there was one thing that I didn't fully understand, a concept that wasn't taught very well in my opinion, and that was the art of worship.

As I grew older and transitioned out of my traditional and orderly missionary Baptist church to attend more contemporary nondenominational churches, I noticed that most of them had replaced a choir with a praise and worship team. The first thirty minutes of every service would be filled with a group of people singing songs about God. There would be a projector screen behind the worship team so that you could follow along with them. Members of the audience would cry, wave their hands, clap, and pour it all out for Jesus.

If I am completely honest, I didn't care for praise and worship and missed being serenaded by the different choirs, so much that I often came to church thirty minutes late to only hear the word. I felt like it didn't "take all that" and I wanted to bypass the hyper-emotional singing. I didn't like how the services made me feel like I didn't have control over my body and my emotions. At my childhood church, no one hardly ever jumped up, fell out, shouted, ran around the room, or laid out face to the ground. I would think to myself "man they must be going through something to be doing all that."

In college, I attended a revival service at the invitation from a classmate and my life was forever changed. I knew that I was a "dreamer" and that there was a chance that I was "prophetic," but I didn't have context or understand. God was already doing a number on me and was sending me back to back visions and signs; I figured that by going to this revival that It would "activate" and help me understand what I had been experiencing since I was a child. One service during praise and worship, I let go, and for the first time, I worshiped. I went down to the altar with the other attendees laid out for prayer and worshiped as I had never worshiped before. That day, I became spirit filled and began to speak in tongues.

Through the years, I became more submitted to the idea of worship, as I remember how it activated the gift of tongues in me. I allowed the spirit to move in my body during service and in my personal worship and began to hear and understand the word of God clearer than ever. It was a pivotal turning point in my relationship with God and brought me to a higher dimension.

Every Christian believer must praise and worship God because it:

- Is an act of surrender and submission
- Puts the focus on God and off of us
- Helps us to get out of our own way and allow God to move
- Celebrates God's goodness and mercy
- Usher's in the presence of God and his angels
- Allows us to hear from God
- Is our personal sacrifice to God
- Forces us to let go of control

You can worship God in your way, either by listening, singing, or dancing to your favorite gospel or Christian song, or audibly giving honor and praise to God. I challenge you to spend one - two minutes each day in praise and worship and watch how God works miracles in your life and your business.

Lord, I will exalt you and praise your name, for in perfect faithfulness you have done wonderful things, things planned long ago. [Isaiah 25:1]

You, God, are my God, earnestly I seek you; I thirst for you, my whole being longs for you, in a dry and parched land where there is no water. [Psalm 63:1]

Father, I repent for not submitting to worshiping you daily. I ask that you instill in me a heart and hunger to worship you O God.

Show me how to let my guard down if I am guarded. Teach me how to worship in a way that pleases you. Fill me with your Holy Spirit and let him worship in me for you Lord.

I sing to you God, I sing and praise your name. I extol you and rejoice before you. You are my Lord, a father to the fatherless, a defender of the widows, and you are holy. [Psalm 68:4-5]

Father I give praise to you Lord, I proclaim your name. I will make your name known among the nations for what you have done. [Psalm 105:1]

Lord, I bow down in worship, I kneel before you Lord, my maker. [Psalm 95:6] But I trust in your unfailing love; my heart rejoices in your salvation. I will sing your praise Lord for you have been good to me. [Psalm 13:5-6]

I will bless you Lord at all times; your praise will always be on my lips. [Psalm 34:1]

I worship you Lord my God, and your blessing will be on my food and water. You will take away sickness from me. [Exodus 23:25] As long as I have breath, I will praise you, Lord. [Psalm 150:6]

And now to him who can keep me on my feet, standing tall in his bright presence, fresh and celebrating – to my one God, my only Savior, through Jesus Christ, our Master, be glory, majesty, strength, and rule before all time, and now, and to the end of all time. [Jude 1: 24-25]

In Jesus name, I pray, amen.

PRAYER THIRTEEN: PURPOSE

You saw me before I was born. Every day of my life was recorded in your book. Every moment was laid out before a single day had passed.
[Psalm 139:16 NLT]

Early one morning God whispered two words to me in my sleep, those words were submissive will. I had never heard the two words linked together in a phrase, so I asked God to reveal exactly what it meant. We often hear of the two phrases as it concerns God's will - sovereign (perfect) will and permissive (moral) will. These "will's" explain why things happen the way they do on earth.

Everything God does is according to is sovereign will. The creation of all things [Jeremiah 32:17], the way things always fall into place despite the sin and poor decisions we commit, the open doors, blessings, and opportunities we can't explain are all God's sovereign will. his sovereign will is everything in the past, present, and future, and the way he always makes everything good according to his purpose. [Romans 8:28]

God also gives us "free will" also known as his moral or permissive will, and it's what God allows to happen even when it is a sin. It's how we can explain all the injustice and evil that is taking place in our country today. God allows us to make our own decisions and live in our sin despite what the purpose and the plan that he has for us. He can turn our "free will" and transform it into his perfect will. [Genesis 50:20] The beautiful thing about is permissive will, is that no matter the sin we are in, the things we have done, the consequences we may have suffered, as long as you are living, there is still time for God to turn it all around and use it to teach us and ultimately serve his purpose for our lives. [Proverbs 16:4]

Our Father can and will use our free will to teach, groom, and grow us for our next season, but following our free will can be coupled with harsh consequences, suffering, and sometimes aborting our purpose. When his sovereign will and permissive will align in your life, you will be in his submissive will. This is the key to living a blessed, satisfied, purpose-driven and righteous life. You have submitted to his perfect will, your purpose and have dedicated your life to being, doing, and having all that God has for you.

You might wrestle with living in God's submissive will because you may not have not identified God's purpose for your life. If you haven't discovered your purpose it's easy to are aimlessly roam the earth trying to please your fleshly desires, and end up failing to live according to what God wants for your life. When you are walking in your purpose - you are able to receive your generational blessings that were assigned to your bloodline before you were born. [Psalm 112:2-3]

Father God, you created the heavens and earth and put everything in place. You made the world to be lived in and not to be a place of empty chaos. For you are Lord and there is none like you. [Isaiah 45:18] Father you are great and worthy of praise for your greatness is unsearchable. [Psalm 145:3]

Father, I repent for not operating in your submissive will. I ask that you forgive me for not walking completely submitted to your purpose for my life. Father, I know that I may have made plans for my life, based on my earthly desires, but I understand that it is your purpose that will prevail. [Proverbs 19:21]

Lord, I come to you asking that you identify the purpose that you have assigned to my life. You saw me before I was born. Every day of my life was recorded in your book. Every moment was laid out before a single day had passed". [Psalm 139:16]

The purposes of my heart are deep waters, Lord you have the insight, and I ask that you reveal my purpose to me. [Proverbs 20:5]

I ask that you align every aspect of my life to fit according to your purpose including my business, my faith, and my relationships. I know Father, that you can do all things and that my purpose can never be undone. [Job 42:2]

Lord, I thank you for saving me through the blood of Jesus Christ and calling me to live a holy life, not because of anything I have done but because of your own purpose and grace. This grace was given me in Christ Jesus before the beginning of time. [2 Timothy 1:9]

Teach me how to walk in my divine purpose, for I know that you have appointmented me for the very purpose of displaying your power in me and so that your name might be proclaimed in all the earth. [Romans 9:17]

In Jesus name I pray, amen.

PRAYER FOURTEEN: GENERATIONAL BLESSINGS

Their children will be mighty in the land; the generation of the upright will be blessed. Psalm 112:2 NLT]

One day in my sleep the Lord whispered the phrase "generational blessings" to me. At the time, I had heard of "generational wealth," but not "generational blessings." I began to pray and ask God to reveal what it meant and what I was supposed to do with it. God led me to a book "Unlocking Destinies in the Courts of Heaven" by Robert Henderson, and the Lord began to show me my purpose on Earth. My purpose is to unlock generational blessings and inheritance through deliverance and kingdom building, hence why I founded Blessed Profits.

Generational blessings are blessings that are assigned to your bloodline. They are the grace which includes: tools, wisdom, resources, favor, health, and wealth that are available to help you fulfill your divine purpose. How many of you know your divine purpose? Exactly what God has called you to do? We all have a purpose on earth, and God has granted us everything we will ever need to fulfill that purpose. That purpose could be a job, business, a ministry. To release your generational blessings, it is imperative to living a fulfilled Godly life. Deliverance from strongholds is key to releasing your generational blessings.

He has saved us and called us to a holy life—not because of anything we have done but because of his own purpose and grace. This grace was given to us in Christ Jesus before the beginning of time. [2 Timothy 1:9] Our purpose was written in our book of life, and God grants us generational blessings to carry out our purpose.

You saw me before I was born. Every day of my life was recorded in your book. Every moment was laid out before a single day had passed. [Psalm 139:16 NLT]

When you are walking in purpose, everything will seem like is flowing just right. You ever see someone that has found his or her niche, and they appear as if everything is going their way? That's because they probably are walking in their divine purpose! That person isn't special; they are using their God-given generational blessings, grace, favor, etc. to do their God-given purpose. Romans 8:31 says that for if God is with us, who can be against us?

But…. There is one thing that can disrupt you receiving your generational blessings, and that is sin. That sin can show up in a variety of ways and is often associated with generational curses. The devil uses generational curses to stop generational blessings! Fortunately for you, you already broke generational curses a few prayers ago. In fact, every prayer you have prayed has been to get you to this point. For the next few prayers, you will be activating your blessings. You can do this because you broke all curses, you have forgiven yourself and those who have hurt you, you let go of fear, you are going to be obedient to your purpose, and you are grateful for your journeys.

Dear most gracious Heavenly Father. I come to you today as your son/daughter in Christ and I give you honor and praise. I worship you and acknowledge you as the creator of all things. Lord, I claim the authority that you have granted me through the blood of Jesus Christ. [Matthew 28:18-19]

I ask that you release that which was assigned to me and my destiny as it is written in my heavenly book. For you saw me before I was born. Every day of my life was recorded in your book. Every moment was laid out before a single day had

passed." [Psalm 139:16]

I repent of every sin that I've committed that the enemy is using against me to hold up the release of my blessings that you, Father God, have for me. Lord, I repent on behalf of the sins of my bloodline that the enemy might be using against me in the heavenly court.

I command Satan and his conspirators through the blood of Jesus to release right now what is owed to me. Release my healing, release, my inheritance, release my finances, release my marriage/relationships. Satan, you have no right to hold on to what God has for me, for I have repented of every accusation you have against me and I call you out for the liar that you are.

Release, release, release it now in the name of Jesus! Lord, I ask that you demand Satan and his co-conspirators to stop their search and delay and release what you have set aside for me to glorify and uplift your Kingdom.

In Jesus Christ name I pray, amen.

PRAYER FIFTEEN: FAVOR

Let the favor of the Lord our God be upon us. And make the work of our hands stand strong. Yes, make the work of our hands stand strong. [Psalm 90:17 NLT]

Have you ever heard of the phrase "favor ain't fair"? I have no idea where people got this phrase from, but we all have access to favor if we ask for it. Favor is included with generational blessings, and is assessable when you are walking in your God-given purpose. When you are obedient to the will and call of God, you will have favor. I have witnessed the Lord's favor work in my life and for my family.

When God first gave me the vision for Myavana, I knew it was something that I had to pursue. I didn't understand all that I know now, except that the vision was from God. I was immediately obedient and prayed and asked God to show me what I needed to do to bring his vision to life. He led me to contact my partner Candace, who connected us with two other ladies who had a similar idea. Within months after us forming a team we were accepted into a business accelerator program and was given mentors, resources, and an investment of thirty thousand to fund our business. We started Myavana without using any of our own money. I know that was nothing but the favor of God because we didn't have a product at the time, only an idea that we had yet to prove that it worked.

A more recent display of God's favor was for my husband Chris. Chris had been searching for months for a new position that could take care of his family and would free me up to do entrepreneurial and ministry endeavors. He had a passion for analyzing data and found out a few months prior that one of his life purposes was to become a data scientist. Chris took classes to increase his subject matter knowledge, and applied to several positions but was having trouble landing a position that paid well enough doing what he loved to do. God placed it on my heart to write this prayer on favor, and I prayed it for him and sent it to him to pray it as well. We were trusting and believing that the Lord's favor was on him.

The next week my husband had three or more interviews lined up for a data science position with three different companies. Chris ended up landing two offers - one of those offers was at his current job that he didn't even apply for, and it was more than double his salary! My husband was able to get the job he desired, that also met his salary requirements, in the location he wanted - talk about the favor of the Lord! If you are waiting on God's favor to rain down on you, I encourage you to recite this prayer daily until your favor begins to manifest.

Dear Heavenly Father, thank you so much for your divine favor. Thank you for always working things out for my business on my behalf. Thank you for being a way maker when I needed direction. Father God, you are the glory of my strength, and through your favor, I am strengthened. [Psalm 89:17]

Lord, I repent for any misuse of favor that was previously granted by you. Father God, I come to you today to request that you accept me and restore your righteousness in my life. [Job 33:26]

Lord, I ask that you give me favor with both you and people and a good reputation. [Proverbs 3:4]

Let your favor be upon me, and show me your approval and make all of my work efforts successful. [Psalm 90:17]

Father God, grant me favor in my business as you did for Joshua. Allow no one to stand against me as long as I live and serve you. For just like you were with Joshua and Moses, may

you also be with me, for I know that you will never fail me. [Joshua 1:5]

Father God I dedicate my business to you and vow to live an upright and just life, for your word says that you are a sun and a shield and you bestow favor and honor. You do not withhold your favor for those who walk upright. [Psalm 84:11].

I ask that you guide my steps according to who you have called me to be and unlock all favor that was assigned to my divine purpose. For through your divine power, you have granted us all things that pertain to my life and godliness, and through my knowledge of you, as you have called me, you have given me favor so that I may walk in my divine purpose and escape the evil and sinful corruption of the world. [2 Peter 1:3-4]

Lord grant me the favor of Noah, Joseph, Samuel, Joshua, and Moses. In Jesus name I Pray, amen.

PRAYER SIXTEEN: OPEN DOORS

But the one who enters through the gate is the shepherd of the sheep. The gatekeeper opens the gate for him, and the sheep recognize his voice and come to him. He calls his own sheep by name and leads them out. [John 10:2-3 NLT]

In 2015, my family and I set out to start a family business named Minute Weave. My sister in law came up with an idea for a detachable weave system. She presented the idea to me one afternoon, and I agreed to help her create it. I was super excited as I love everything hair and beauty. In one weekend we were able to build a prototype that would serve as a demo unit to prove our weave system worked. It was a pretty novel idea; we attached premium human grade hair to a Velcro strip that could attach to a wig cap. You could create a new look in as little as ten minutes or less.

For the rest of 2015, we perfected the design, and we were able to secure vendors at reasonable wholesale prices for all materials. In 2016 we decided to participate in a crowdfunding pre-order campaign to garner support, press, and funding to launch Minute Weave to consumers. After careful planning, we launched our crowdfunding campaign in May of 2016 with the goal of raising $15,000 to fund our business. We set daily and weekly goals to motivate and push us towards reaching our funding goals.

That same month I attended a women's empowerment dinner where Evangelist Latrice Ryan was the guest speaker. During the dinner, she prophesied and prayed for open doors and expansion for everyone in the room. I gathered what little cash I had and made sure to sow into the word she released to over one hundred women in attendance. I received the word and believed that she was talking about my business.

Later that night my husband and I were headed back to the event center where the dinner was held to help clean up and pack up the decorations. I was in the passenger seat scrolling Facebook, and I see a photo of myself with the Minute Weave unit on posted by Essence Magazine. I did a double take and realized that Essence Magazine had done a write-up on our product and our crowdfunding campaign! I nearly jumped out of my seat. Within the next hour, my notifications were going crazy as new people were signing up to learn more about Minute Weave every minute. Not only were new people signing up to learn more, but people were also donating and purchasing our product. We continued to get consistent signups throughout the campaign and increased our email list by one thousand percent.

Other national news outlets picked up our story, and our brand became nationally known in less than thirty days. The open door prophetic word manifested within twenty four hours, we met our funding goal and completed a successful pre-order campaign. Because we created a plan and were willing to take the first step, God had an open door ready and waiting for us to walk through it. I challenge you to read this prayer and sow an extra seed into a ministry of your choice with an expectant heart for every door before you to open.

Dear Heavenly Father, you are awesome, you are righteous, you are merciful, you are above all. I thank you for loving me enough that you have already laid out a purpose and a plan for my life. Lord, I love you, honor you, and I give you all the praise and glory, for there is none like you. You are the creator of every door, of every opportunity that I will ever need.

Lord, I repent for not walking through previous doors that you have opened for me due to fear, not feeling good enough, or not being prepared. I ask that you re-open doors that I may have

closed in my ignorance.

Father, you are holy, you are true, and you hold the key. You open doors that no one will shut, and you shut doors that no one can open. For you know the work that I have to do, and I ask that you put before me an open door in which no one can shut. I acknowledge that I am powerless without you and I vow to obey you and will not deny you, Lord. [Revelation 3:7-8]

Lord give me the key to the house of David—the highest position in the royal court. When I open the door, no one will be able to close them; when I close a door, no one will be able to open them.

Father, I thank you for being my doorkeeper. I will pay attention to your voice and listen when you call so that I may enter the correct doors that you have for me. [John 10:2-3] I ask that you shut all doors that are not for me and redirect my path.

I prophesy open doors of opportunity, advancement, and acceleration for my business before the end of the year and I thank you for giving me my purpose. In Jesus name I pray, amen.

PRAYER SEVENTEEN: INHERITANCE

I will confirm my covenant with you and your descendants after you, from generation to generation. This is the everlasting covenant: I will always be your God and the God of your descendants after you.
[Genesis 17:7 NLT]

Did you know that it is outside the will of God for you to struggle financially? God desires for your entire generation, your bloodline to be blessed and wealthy. For the Bible says "Their children will be successful everywhere; an entire generation of godly people will be blessed. They themselves will be wealthy, and their good deeds will last forever". [Psalm 112:2-3 NLT]. While you are living on Earth, it is your duty as a child of God to create generational wealth.

A good person leaves an inheritance for their children's children, but a sinner's wealth is stored up for the righteous. [Proverbs 13:22 NLT]

This isn't just some false, exaggerated prosperity teaching, but it is mandated in the word of God; For money is the answer to all things. [Ecclesiastes 10:19] If we are Kingdom Entrepreneurs, we most certainly need money to build God's Kingdom and meet the needs of his church and his people.

Awhile back I used to joke about not having a rich uncle to help me through all of my entrepreneurial endeavors. I believed that I had to pave the way for my family and generations to come for me to be wealthy. I was willing to work as hard as I needed to make sure it would happen. When I first started Myavana, I worked and worked and worked often forgoing sleep to make sure that I accomplished all my tasks. At the time, I only had a husband and no kids, so I figured I could work as long as I wanted or needed to. Sometimes I'd only get 4-5 hours sleep at night, get up and go to my full-time job, then head over to my other office to build Myavana. I was following the popular saying I'll sleep when I die.

I found out years later that I was not honoring God the way I should, for the Bible says:

> *It is useless for you to work so hard from early morning until late at night, anxiously working for food to eat; for God gives rest to his loved ones. [Psalm 127:2 NLT]*

I thought that by working hard I was going to be rich! You read all of those stories about millionaires and billionaires only sleeping for four hours at a time, but what you don't read about is how often they are doing it or if and when they are taking vacations and breaks.

It is God's will that I not only prosper but that I don't kill myself in the process. I also found out that I am an heir to the richest man that ever walked this earth, Abraham. Do you remember that song you sang in Bible school as a child "Father Abraham, had many sons, many sons had Father Abraham, I am one of them, and so are you, so let's just praise the Lord - right arm, left arm...." God promised Abraham that his descendants great wealth.

> *I will make you very fruitful; I will make nations of you, and kings will come from you. I will establish my covenant as an everlasting covenant between me and you and your descendants after you for the generations to come, to be your God and the God of your descendants after you. The whole land of Canaan, where you now reside as a foreigner, I will give as an everlasting possession to you and your descendants after you; and I will be their God. [Genesis 17:6-8 NLT]*

You might be wondering, "Well how is that? What qualifies me to be a son or daughter of Abraham?" Romans 4:16 says:

Therefore, the promise comes by faith so that it may be by grace and may be guaranteed to all Abraham's offspring—not only to those who are of the law but also to those who have the faith of Abraham. He is the Father of us all. [Romans 4:16 NIV]

Because you are a follower and believer of Jesus Christ, you are one of Abraham's descendants. Galatians 3:29 and Hebrews 1:2 declares:

And if you belong to Christ, then you are Abraham's descendants, heirs according to promise. [Galatians 3:29 NLT]

And now in these final days, he has spoken to us through his Son. God promised everything to the Son as an inheritance, and through the Son he created the universe. [Hebrews 1:2 NLT]

It's that simple, if you have accepted Jesus Christ in your heart, then you have an inheritance assigned to you. You can be wealthy, you can create generational wealth, and it is your inheritance to prosper.

Most gracious Heavenly Father, I thank you for all that you are and for all that you do. I thank you for being the King of Kings, the author of my destiny, and the giver of my inheritance.

I acknowledge that all that is or will ever be belongs to you. For Psalm 89:11 says: The heavens are Yours, the earth also is Yours; The world and all that is in it, You have founded and established them. Thank you, God, for sending your son Jesus Christ, for whom you have appointed an heir to all things including the wealth and riches of the earth. [Hebrews 1:2]

I have accepted Jesus Christ in my heart and I believe that he is your son, sent by you to redeem me from my sins. Father God, I claim the rightful ownership of my inheritance as granted to me, the descendant of Abraham. [Genesis 17:6-8]

For Galatians 3:29 says that if you belong to Christ, then you are Abraham's descendants, heirs according to promise. I repent of my sins and the sins of my ancestors, and I ask that through the bloodshed from your son Jesus Christ that our sins and the sins

of my grandfather's grandfathers be washed away. I also repent on behalf of, and I forgive any negative words that I have spoken or negative words that were spoken against me by those who have authority in my life and your kingdom. I ask that you strike down the lies and accusations that my adversary may be using against me in the heavenly courts. [Revelation 12:10]

For you have canceled the record of the charges against me and took it away by nailing it to the cross. [Colossians☐ ☐2:14☐] I ask that you loose my generational blessings to me now and I prophesy that my children will be successful everywhere; an entire generation of godly people will be blessed. They themselves will be wealthy, and their good deeds will last forever. [Psalm 112:2-3]. I declare that every resource, money, wisdom, favor, and grace will be released to me now in Jesus name amen.

PRAYER EIGHTEEN: WISDOM

How much better to get wisdom than gold, and good judgment than silver! [Proverbs 16:16 NLT]

Most of us choose entrepreneurship because we not only get to do something we love doing, but we can also get paid for it. When I started entrepreneurship in 2012, I knew I loved beauty and hair care. I got my degrees in chemical engineering because I wanted to design and create hair and beauty products for women of color. When the Lord placed on my heart to start Myavana, It was a no-brainer that I would pursue the opportunity. I had a chance to turn my passion into profit, and making money was a big deal.

We were first-time entrepreneurs who were excited to be the faces of black women in technology, but making money was my motive behind every decision. As we struggled to figure out our business model, I remember praying to God "Dear Lord; PLEASE make this work! Help us to get all these sign-ups on our website/app/services (we changed our business model three times). Pretty PLEASE! In Jesus name, amen". The prayer didn't go exactly like that every time, but you get it! I knew we needed the people to get the money to get the next investment to get acquired. We were trying to sell a multi-million dollar company.

I realized later that I was asking God for all of the wrong things. Now I am not saying that my prayer shouldn't have included getting people to sign up for our website/app/service, but there was something far greater that I should've asked for, and that is wisdom. More specifically, I should have asked for wisdom like King Solomon. [1 Kings 4:29] God came to King Solomon in a dream and asked him what he wanted. [1 Kings 3:5] Solomon could have asked for anything - wealth, healing, power, influence, etc. but instead, he asked for wisdom.

Now, O Lord my God, you have made me king instead of my father, David but I am like a little child who doesn't know his way around. And here I am in the midst of your own chosen people, a nation so great and numerous they can not be counted! Give me an understanding heart so that I can govern your people well and know the difference between right and wrong. For who by himself is able to govern this great people of yours? [1 Kings 3:7-9 NLT]

How many of us can relate to King Solomon? You may have just started your business, or you may have come to a point where you are spinning your wheels trying to figure out what to do and where to go. It's easy to result to Lord, give me XYZ so that I can get to the money!! Instead, recite the words that Solomon said to God over your business.

God was so pleased by Solomon's request and the fact that he didn't ask for wealth, or long life, or retaliation against his enemies that He granted Solomon with wisdom, wisdom that no one else has had, and that no one else would ever have. In addition to wisdom, God also promised riches, fame, and long life! [1 Kings 3:10-14] King Solomon's request not only blessed him and his family but his entire kingdom!! [1 Kings 4:20] The Kingdom depends on your wisdom to bless the people!

Dear Heavenly Father, I come to you thankful and appreciative of you. I honor you and love you Lord. Father teach me to be wise and to understand your ways as I strive to live an honorable life doing good deeds with humility that comes from God granted wisdom. [James 3:13]

For your foolishness Lord, is wiser than the wisest of any wisdom that I may possess. [1 Corinthians 1:25]

God I ask that you administer your wisdom for my faith is in you and you alone. [James 1:5]

I no longer rely on my own understanding, Lord, and I trust you with all of my heart! [Proverbs 3:5] I repent for trying to figure it all out, without seeking your face and your wisdom in all things.

Father, I know that it is much better to gain wisdom than gold and to get insight than silver. [Proverbs 16:16]

Lord, give me spiritual wisdom and insight so that I can grow in your knowledge. I pray that my heart will be flooded with light to understand the hope you have given me and the greatness of your power God. [Ephesians 1: 16-19]

Give me the wisdom to make the most of every relationship and every opportunity that is before me. [Colossians 4:5-6]

Proverbs 3:13 says - blessed are those who find wisdom, those who gain understanding. Give me the wisdom to properly manage all the affairs of my business, including my finances, time, decision making, and resources.

Lord grant me the wisdom of King Solomon, so that I may be wise beyond my years and give me an understanding heart so that I can govern your (insert business here) well and know the difference between right and wrong. For who by himself can govern this (insert business/request here) of yours? [1 Kings 3:11-12] In Jesus name I pray amen.

PRAYER NINETEEN: GRACE

May God give you more and more grace and peace as you grow in your knowledge of God and Jesus our Lord. [2 Peter 1:2 NLT]

It wasn't until recently that I began to understand God's grace. I was familiar with the concept of grace, as I had heard about it as a child growing up in church. The term was mostly used to describe the gift that was given to us through the death of Jesus Christ that allowed us redemption for our sins and put us under a new law. As with several "Bible concepts" I didn't fully understand how it applied to my personal life, let alone my business. Grace is given to us freely and isn't something we can earn or buy. It is the exact opposite of karma - you don't get it because you deserve it.

Matthew 20:1-16 is a well-known parable about God's grace. Jesus makes a comparison of the Kingdom of Heaven to a landowner who goes out early looking to hire workers for his vineyard. The landowner decides that he will pay each worker the normal daily wage and would send them out to work. At nine o'clock in the morning, the landowner passed through the marketplace and saw a group of people standing around doing nothing. He hires them and tells them he would pay them a daily wage at the end of the day. They all agreed and left to work the vineyard. The man found another group of people doing nothing and hired them to work his vineyard at booth noon and three o'clock. At five o'clock the landowner returned to the vineyard and saw more people standing around, and he asked them why they were not working. They replied that no one had hired them.

The landowner asked them to go and join the others that were working in his vineyard.

Later that evening he told his foreman to call all of his workers in and pay them, beginning with the last workers first. Those that were hired at five o'clock were paid a full day's wage. When those that were hired first came to collect their payment, they assumed that they would be paid more, but were paid a full day's wage just like the others. They protested their wage saying that it was unfair that the people who only worked one hour were paid just as much as them, because they were working in the hot scorching heat all day. The landowner reminded them that they agreed to work for a full day's wage and that he could do whatever he pleased with his money. He decided to pay everyone the same and commanded them to take their payment and to leave. He asked them if it was against the law and if they were jealous that he was kind to everyone. The story concludes with the verse:

So those who are last now will be first then, and those who are first will be last. [Matthew 20:16 NLT]

By now you have probably realized that money in this story is symbolic for God's grace.

How many of us can identify with that story? I couldn't understand why others in business "who just started" were doing "better" than me. I mean I have paid my dues, I have burned the midnight oil, I was committed to the process. But it appeared as though others "just popped up on the scene" and were further along than me, it just wasn't fair. This produced bitterness and then jealousy for how God blessed others, and I started to believe that God had forgotten about me. I was soon reminded that God never directed me to work as hard as I did. I was working and hustling and grinding trying to make my own way when I never asked God exactly what and how I should be working. For when you are doing the work of God his yoke is easy, and his burden is light. [Matthew 11:30] I was working outside of God's grace and was feeling burned out, frustrated and rejected - this was not the will of God.

I was also reminded of the grace that God had extended me over and over in my business - the fact that my co-founders and I were able launch Myavana without spending any of our own money, and how we were able to sufficiently fund our company having raised hundreds of thousands of dollars. Every single time God needed us to accomplish a task, there was an amount of unique favor and grace that accompanied it. And lastly, I was reminded that we all have different journeys and that I could not compare myself to others and how God graced others to do what he called them to accomplish. I needed to celebrate them instead of becoming envious of how God chose to bless them.

Grace is not just for me when I need it, but God gives it freely to everyone who needs it. When God is in it, grace will be attached to it. You can't earn it; you can't purchase it; you can't take it from someone else. If you are overworked, tired, and have yet to yield results, it's time to move out of your own way, and ask for God's grace to carry you through.

Father God, I thank you for sending your son Jesus Christ to die on the cross for my sins so that gift of grace may rest freely on me. For your grace is all that I need and your power is made perfect in my weakness. [2 Corinthians 12:9]

Lord, I approach your throne of grace with confidence so that I may find mercy and grace to help me in my time of need. [Hebrews 4:16]

I am grateful that sin is no longer my master, and that I am no longer under the law, but under your grace. [Romans 6:14]

Father, I vow to use the gifts that you have given me to faithfully serve others as a good steward of the grace you have granted me. [1 Peter 4:10]

I repent for trying to rely on my own strength and not relying on your grace to get me through. I also repent for feeling bitter or jealous for how you decided to grace others. I will be grateful for the grace that you have given me. For grace has been extended to each one of us as through your son, Jesus. [Ephesians 4:7]

Lord, I ask that grace and peace be given to me in abundance

for all things including my business, through the knowledge of you and your son Jesus Christ. [2 Peter 1:2]

Father, I thank you for giving me more grace daily as I remain humble, for you favor the humble and oppose the proud. [James 4:6] In Jesus name, I pray amen.

PRAYER TWENTY: INCREASE

And though you started with little, you will end with much. [Job 8:7 NLT]

Our Father is not a God of lack. He desires for us to live an abundant life full of everything we could ever need. There are several instances in the Bible where the Lord provided overflow for his sons and daughters when they needed it most. Increase is a critical part of the spiritual circle of life, and God uses it as a tool to build his Kingdom. [2 Corinthians 9:10] Just think, if God can give you, as a Christian business owner increase, how it can benefit followers of Christ. When God increases your influence, you can proclaim the word of God to a larger audience. When God increases your finances, you can tithe and sow more into your church and Kingdom initiatives. When God increases your faith, you can decree and declare a thing and so shall it be, and when you have proven to be faithful and grateful with what God has granted you, your increase is around the corner. It is okay to desire more than what you currently have because when you have more, you can do more.

Increase is demonstrated in one of my favorite Bible stories in Matthew 14:13-21, Jesus feeds five thousand. We know from this story that Jesus was headed to be alone to mourn the death of John the Baptist, but his followers heard where he was headed and traveled from many towns to see him so they could be healed. After some time, everyone grew hungry, and the disciples wanted to send the people away so that they could buy food for themselves. But Jesus instructed his disciples to them saying "They do not need to go away, you give them something to eat". [Matthew 14:16] The disciples responded that they only had five loaves of bread and two fish - they had no idea how they could feed an entire crowd of people with so little. Jesus told the disciples to bring the loaves and fish to him and instructed the crowds of people to have a seat in the grass. Jesus took the five loaves and two fish, looked up toward heaven, and blessed them. He then broke the loaves into pieces and gave the bread to his disciples, who distributed it to the people. Everyone ate as much as they wanted and the disciples picked up twelve baskets of leftovers. About five thousand men, women, and children were fed in that day.

This parable is so rich because it outlines how God uses us, his disciples to feed his children. Jesus could have waved his hand and made bread fall out of the sky for everyone to eat, but he didn't. He instructed his disciples to be the vessel to feed the families. The disciples brought Jesus all that they had and Jesus told the people to sit and wait - there are people assigned to your increase. He took what the disciples gave them and looked up toward heaven - through the blood of Jesus Christ, God is the source of all increase. Jesus gave the bread back to the disciples, and it was more than enough to feed everyone there, in fact, they had twelve baskets of leftovers after feeding over five thousand men, women, and children. It is time to submit your business, ministry, brand, nonprofit to God so that he may increase you to serve his people.

Most gracious Heavenly Father, I thank you for being my provider, a waymaker, a healer, and much more. I honor you, worship you, and lift up your heavenly and holy name. I acknowledge that my increase comes from you and that I shall never want. [Psalm 23:1]

For it is you, Lord, who supplies seed to the sower and bread for food. You will provide and multiply my seed for sowing and increase my harvest. [2 Corinthians 9:10]

Lord, I repent for not always being a good steward over my increase, I ask that you forgive me for mishandling what you have granted me.

May you Father, the God of my ancestors, increase my business a thousand times and bless me as you have promised! [Deuteronomy 1:11]

Father, I vow to sow and give back to your Kingdom via my tithe and offering for your word says give, and it will be given to you. A good measure, pressed down, shaken together and running over, will be poured into my lap. For with the measure I use, it will be measured unto me. [Luke 6:38]

Lord as I honor you with my wealth by giving to you first, will you bring overflow to my business. [Proverbs 3:9-10]

Lord, I ask that you increase my money, influence, resources, favor, grace, customers, products, and faith. May my business be planted in good soil to produce good crop and allow it to multiply thirty, sixty, and one hundred times. [Mark 4:8]

Before the end of this year, Father I ask that every seed I have sown be blessed and returned to me one hundredfold. [Genesis 26:12]

Father, I ask that the days to come will be filled with increase, [Job 8:7] and that my family and I flourish. [Psalm 115:14] In Jesus name I pray, amen.

PRAYER TWENTY ONE: PROTECTION

God is our refuge and strength, always ready to help in times of trouble. [Psalm 46:1 NLT]

Have you ever hoped, prayed, and desired something so bad you ached? You might have just known that it was going to be everything you needed to help you achieve next level success. There have been many instances in my life and business where there was a seemingly remarkable opportunity presented to me and I desperately wanted to come to pass because it was going to "put me on" so to speak.

In the summer of 2016, I was contacted by three different production companies to share my story via a reality T.V. series on national television. I had already played this song and dance in previous years, as I had been contacted at least three to four other times. What was different about this instance was that the show would feature my immediate family - my husband, my daughter, my son (I was pregnant at the time) and me. I had already lost so much that year, including burying my Nana and my Dad, that I thought it would be a perfect way to end the year on a high note. And let's be honest, I wanted the opportunity to have national fame.

After several interviews with the show coordinators and network producers, we were selected as one of four families to participate in a new show that was already picked up by a national cable network, and filming would begin around the birth of my son Cue. They wanted to share the story of a young married couple pursuing entrepreneurship while trying to raise a family. I was so excited to share my story and couldn't wait to get started. They sent over the contracts for us to sign and as I begin to read each line, my spirit didn't sit well with what I was reading.

I contacted my longtime college friend who is also an attorney and asked her to review the contracts and got her advice on if this was going to be an opportunity or a mistake. Once reviewed she informed me that signing the contracts as is would be a huge mistake for my family and my career. The news crushed me. We attempted to get the contracts modified to better suit my interests, but unfortunately, they weren't willing to comprise.

I was devastated, I had convinced myself that this was my "big break" and that I needed this "opportunity." I'd already been on national television a few times for short media segments, and I saw the positive impact that it had on our company and knew that a recurring spot television would elevate my brand even higher. It wasn't until months later that I realized that appearing on a reality television show in that season of our lives was a terrible idea. I had so many issues that God needed to purge from me in private, that I couldn't imagine going through my purification process publicly.

God was protecting me from myself by not allowing me to participate in what appeared to be a great business opportunity but probably would have redirected me from my path and my purpose. What looked like rejection was God's protection. I am so happy that I spent time away from the spotlight to focus on restoration, healing, and deliverance for me, my husband, our marriage, and our finances. The remarkable thing about God is that he not only protects us from outside danger and harm, he also protects us from the plots and schemes the enemy creates that is a direct attempt to abort us from our purpose.

Father God, you are beautiful, you are awesome, you are my protector, you are my healer, you are a peacekeeper, and much more. I honor you, worship you, and love you with all of my heart and soul. I thank you for loving me, despite me. You keep me safe Lord, and I find refuge in you. [Psalm 16:1]

Even though the world is full of uncertainties and evildoers, I

will be strong and courageous. I will not be afraid or terrified because of them, for you are with me Father, you will never leave or forsake me. [Deuteronomy 31:6] I have put on my full armor of God so that I can stand against the devil's schemes. [Ephesians 6:11]

Father, I repent for not allowing you to protect me in all things and for doubting that you are with me. I also repent for fearing man and believing that they have more power than you.

Father your name is a fortified tower; the righteous run to it and are safe. [Proverbs 18:10] It is better that I take refuge in you Lord than to trust in humans. [Psalm 118:8] I thank you, Father, for being my refuge and strength, and an ever-present help in trouble. [Psalm 46:1]

Father your word says that no weapon formed against me will prevail and that I will refute every tongue that accuses me. This is my heritage as a servant of you Lord, and this is my vindication from you. [Isaiah 54:17]

Lord, I will get out of my way and allow you to work in me. I will not attempt to become the source of my protection for I will be still and allow you to fight for me and my business. [Exodus 14:14]

Lord, I ask that you cover my family, my business, my finances, my purpose, my relationships and my (insert anything that isn't listed). Father, I ask that you loose thousands of angels to protect me and keep me safe from harm. [Matthew 26:53]

Rescue me from my enemies, O God. Protect me from those who have come to destroy me. [Psalm 59:1]

In times of trouble, may the Lord answer my cry. May the name of the God of Jacob keep me safe from all harm. [Psalm 20:1]
In Jesus name I pray, amen.

PRAYER TWENTY TWO: RESOURCES

And God will generously provide all you need. Then you will always have everything you need and plenty left over to share with others. [2 Corinthians 9:8 NLT]

I have always been good at finding resources. Anytime I have ever needed something to complete a particular task, by the grace of God, I have what I need. I did and continued to do one simple thing, and it has never failed me. I ask God for exactly what I need. When I learn about an opportunity, I ask my Father first to show me how I can obtain the resources to participate in the opportunity.

In high school, I applied to attend college out of state. As most of you know there are significant fees when not attending school in your home state. I'd always wanted to live in Atlanta, and was determined to make it my home. I applied for every single scholarship I could get my hands on. I didn't care if it was for a hundred or a hundred thousand dollars, I was going to apply. I didn't care if I met the requirements or not, I was going to apply. I spent hours daily visiting school counselors and searching the internet, and my diligence paid off. My first year of college was covered entirely. I continued to follow the same method while in school and racked up thousands of dollars. One year I had so many scholarships that I ended up sending back $5000 because I had maxed out on student aid.

I used the same methods to fund and build my businesses. I have mentioned several times how I cofounded Myavana without investing any of my money. Every single time we needed something, rather it was office space, lawyers, mentors, staff, and tools, God always delivered right on time. We would think about what we needed, ask God for the resource, and get to work. We didn't sit around and wait for the resources to fall out of the sky, we proactively searched for what we needed, and were open to receiving it, even in ways we never expected.

If our Father created the heavens, the earth, and all that is in existence, then surely he can give you everything you need to position you for success. The problem with most believers is that they don't trust that God is going to supply what they need when they need it. God has a purpose and a plan for your life, and he has already laid out every resource you would ever need to fulfill that purpose. When you are chasing God's purpose and not money, you will live a life of abundance and overflow.

Is there something that you know you are purposed to do or start? Have you not started it or completed the project because you are unsure of where the resources are going to come from? Write out exactly what you desire and make a list of all the resources that you believe you need to get started. Afterwards, pray and ask God for every single item on your list.

Heavenly Father, I acknowledge you as the creator of the heavens and the earth, and all that inhabits it. [Genesis 1:1] Just as you are the creator of all things I know that you have the power to supply all my needs.

I repent Father for not coming to you in my times of need and for relying on my own strength. I also repent for asking, but not having faith that you will grant me the resources to walk in my purpose. I also repent for not using the resources that you have previously given me due to unbelief, laziness, or misuse.

Father I ask that you give me everything I need for (list business, project, ministry, etc.). [Matthew 6:11]

Heavenly Father you already know what I need. I am seeking

the Kingdom of God above all else, I am living righteously, and I have faith that you will give me everything I need. [Matthew 6:32-33]

Thank you, God, for supplying my every need for my business according to your riches in glory in Christ Jesus. [Philippians 4:19]

And God, you can make all resources come in abundance to me, so that I may always have complete sufficiency in my business, and have an abundance for every good work and act of charity. [2 Corinthians 9:8]

I can do all things through you Lord, who strengthens and empowers me to fulfill my purpose. [Philippians 4:13]

I thank you in advance that every resource that I could ever need is already made available to me. for (list business, project, ministry, etc.)

I acknowledge that I am not qualified to claim anything as coming from me, but my resources and qualifications come from you God. [2 Corinthians 3:5] In Jesus name I pray, amen.

PRAYER TWENTY THREE: LONGEVITY

He asked you to preserve his life, and you granted his request.
The days of his life stretch on forever. [Psalm 21:4NLT]

It's one thing to start a business, but it's another to have a long living and thriving business. We hear the statistics; most small businesses fail within the first five years. Although this may be true, it is not the desire of our Father. God desires for us to have three generations of wealth set aside for our children's children [Proverbs 13:22], what better way to do this by leaving a business as an inheritance for our bloodline.

I've talked immensely about my successes in business, but it is important to discuss my failures. I have experienced business failure a few times. My most recent experience was with the family business Minute Weave. At the time, I didn't understand that the spirit of death was lingering over the business as my father in law suffered a massive heart attack the day we planned to launch the pre-order campaign. Our issue wasn't that we had a failed product or a failed business idea, it was we couldn't agree on how to do business together.

Even though the success, the sales, the national media coverage, we struggled to agree on the smallest things. There were was so much anger, fear, bitterness, jealousy, anxiety; you name it. It was also revealed that we had a generational curse over our finances, we were doomed before we even started. The enemy set out to destroy our business and our family and won.

I experienced so many ungodly emotions after the business shut

77

down, I felt like a loser and a failure. I was living with so much unforgiveness and bitterness that my chest and body would ache every time I would think about all that had transpired. It was one of the most hurtful experiences I'd ever had, but it taught me the importance of covering your business in prayer and is the foundation for my ministry Blessed Profits. I pray that each of you never experiences painful business failure and that your business and life are filled with life, love, and happiness.

Father God, you are perfect, you are holy, you are love, and you are righteous. Your name is above all names [Philippians 2:9], and I bless and honor you, Lord.

I repent for all sins that I have committed both known and unknown. I thank you that through the blood of your son Jesus Christ, my sins have been redeemed. [Ephesians 1:7]

Lord, I repent for any negative words I have spoken over my business and other businesses. From this day forward I will keep from speaking evil from my lips and refrain from telling lies so that my business will be long living and happy. [1 Peter 3:10] I ask that every negative word is replaced with a blessing. I will bless those I have cursed.

Lord, I thank you for showing me my divine purpose and allowing me to serve you through my business. I thank you for releasing anything that has been held up in the heavens that would help my business succeed. I thank you for unlocking my generational blessings that are assigned to my bloodline, including all the favor, grace, and resources.

Father, I thank you for cleaning my bloodline and doing away with all curses that sought out to destroy my purpose. I thank you for giving me a sound mind and ridding me from fear, anxiety, rejection, doubt, and unforgiveness.

I thank you for increasing my faith and strengthening me emotionally so that I can withstand any and all attacks from the enemy and from those who seek to destroy my purpose. I thank you, Father, that you have released my inheritance, as a believer in Jesus Christ.

Lord, you have given me every single thing that I could ever need to be successful and to experience longevity in my business. I cancel all spirits of murder that would seek to abort my purpose and cause me to shorten the lifespan of my business.

I thank you for the wisdom you have granted me to ensure that the days of my business will be multiplied and that years have been added to my life. [Proverbs 9:11] Through my God-given wisdom my business will have long life, riches, and honor. [Proverbs 3:16]

Father, I vow to honor you and your commandments, and I am submitted to your will and your word. Through my obedience, my business will experience a long and satisfying lifespan. [Proverbs 3:1-2]

Lord, preserve the life of my business, may the days of my business stretch on forever. [Psalm 21:4] In Jesus name, I pray, amen.

PRAYER TWENTY FOUR: FAMILY

But the love of the Lord remains forever with those who fear him.
His salvation extends to the children's children. [Psalm 103:17
NLT]

I enter into every new year with an expectant heart for God to do something amazing in my life and for my business. I proudly proclaim that this is "my year" and that I am going to achieve all of my wildest dreams and be successful in all that I do. I felt like this in 2016 as my family, and I was making significant transitions and taking major risks in hopes of building generational wealth for our family. We sold our house, took the cash and paid off all debt, downsized tremendously, started our family business Minute Weave, and my husband started a new job.

The exact opposite happened. I experienced the most loss, financial strain, and stress then I'd ever experienced in my entire life. We downsized our home and moved into an inexpensive apartment, but somehow had more bills. My husband made more money, but we didn't have enough to cover everything. We paid off all our credit but ended up back in debt. My husband started a new job but ended up getting fired eight months later. We bought a new condo but had to wipe out all of our 401Ks just to purchase and stay in it. We launched a new business, only for it to shut down months later. My birth father and my Nana died within days from each other, my husband was diagnosed with chronic depression, and my father in law suffered a massive heart attack. I was stressed, unhappy, bitter, angry, jealous, frustrated, and every other negative emotion you could ever feel. It was like no matter what we did; we would only get but so far until we either plateaued or failed.

I wasn't used to failure and failing, and my husband joked that maybe I married into a cursed family. I quickly brushed it off with a chuckle and told him that wasn't possible and that we were just going through a rough season. I find out at the beginning of 2017 that my husband was correct. God confirmed it to me in a series of dreams, vision, and revelations. I knew that if we wanted to experience real success that we needed to protect, bless, and cleanse our bloodline.

Quickly after finding out that we were indeed cursed, I listed out every single sin, sickness, or affliction that my family and I experienced. I began to repent for everything on that list and asked God for forgiveness, and I asked my husband do the same thing. Within weeks our lives started to change for the better. New jobs, new money, healing, deliverance, and favor started coming our way. It was proof that we had cleansed our bloodline, were now walking in God's favor, and that the curses had been lifted.

Father, I give you thanks because you are near and never far. I will tell everyone of all of the wonderful things you have done for me. [Psalm 75:1] Lord I will praise your name forever and ever for you have all the wisdom and power. [Daniel 2:20] God, I thank you for being my father, and a father to those who are fatherless. For I am the clay, and you are the potter. I am the work of your glorious hands. [Isaiah 64:8]

Lord, I proclaim my love for you. I believe and trust in your will and that our son Jesus Christ has redeemed me from my sins. As a result, I am saved, and my family is saved. [Acts 16:31] Father I ask that you bless my family (list family member) in all that they do. May you cover them and protect them.

I pray that no plan or attack of the enemy will prosper and that my family will be kept safe from harm as I do your work. For I am working not only for myself, but for my bloodline, as I desire to create at least three generations of wealth for me, my

children, and my grandchildren. [Proverbs 13:22]

I repent for the sins of my family and my bloodline both known and unknown, and I ask that through the blood of Jesus Christ I be redeemed and cleared from all sins. [Ephesians 1:7] I also intercede for and repent on behalf of (list family member) for (list known sin) and ask that their name be cleared from anything the adversary might be using against them in the courts of heaven.

Father, I ask that you cancel any word curses that were spoken against me by my family and people in authority with the intention of thwarting my purpose.

Lord, I repent for any curses I have spoken over members of my family including (list any negative words you have said about or to family members) especially those aimed at tearing and destroying their purpose.

I ask that all generational curses that seek to annihilate my family bloodline including: sickness, mental illness, cancer, diabetes, poverty, anger, malice, pride, death, abortions, miscarriages, fatherlessness, homosexuality, gender confusion and (name anything that wasn't listed) be cast out from every family member and sent to the abyss never to return again.

Lord, we cast out the spirit of Jezebel and Ahab that may have manifested in my bloodline seeking to destroy my family and me. [Revelation 2:20]

Father may my bloodline be successful everywhere, and my entire generation is blessed. [Psalm 112:2]

Lord, I ask that any attempt made by the enemy to attack the men in my bloodline cease in the name of Jesus. May my family name live on forever through the end of time.

I decree and declare that my children, cousins, aunts, uncles, sisters, brothers, mother, father, and grandparents are covered under by the blood of Jesus Christ, blessed and prosperous. As I am blessed so they will also be blessed. In Jesus name I pray, amen.

PRAYER TWENTY FIVE: PRODUCTS & SERVICES

When she told the man of God what had happened, he said to her, "Now sell the olive oil and pay your debts, and you and your sons can live on what is left over." [2 Kings 4:7 NLT]

You are not a business owner if you aren't selling anything. You are only a hobbyist because a business must have an exchange of products or services with money. God uses the sale of products and services to provide us what we need by sowing into the business owner who is selling them. Each time you purchase a product from someone you are sowing money into the seller's family, investors, employees, etc. If you can figure out the right goods and services to offer, you and your family will never go hungry.

Some of you may be struggling to find the right products to sell, but I want you to be encouraged. God has gifted every single one of us with oil - something that we have and do naturally that can be used as a resource for the Kingdom. Your oil (what you have to offer) is beautifully illustrated in one of my favorite Bible stories from 2 Kings 4:1-7, Elisha Helps the Poor Widow.

One day the widow of a member of the group of prophets came to Elisha and cried out, "My husband who served you is dead, and you know how he feared the Lord. But now a creditor has come, threatening to take my two sons as slaves." "What can I do to help you?" Elisha asked. "Tell me, what do you have in the house?" "Nothing at all, except a flask of olive oil," she replied. And Elisha said, "Borrow as many empty jars as you can from your friends and neighbors. Then go into your house with your sons and shut the door behind you.

Pour olive oil from your flask into the jars, setting each one aside when it is filled." So she did as she was told. Her sons kept bringing jars to her, and she filled one after another. Soon every container was full to the brim! "Bring me another jar," she said to one of her sons. "There aren't any more!" he told her. And then the olive oil stopped flowing. When she told the man of God what had happened, he said to her, "Now sell the olive oil and pay your debts, and you and your sons can live on what is left over." [2 Kings 4:1-7 NLT]

There are a few discussion points that can be extracted from this story. First, Elisha helped the widow to realize that she was already enough and that she had everything she needed. She didn't have to go and invest in a massive marketing campaign, spend money on expensive graphics, pay thousands of dollars to a business coach, or purchase a thousand dollar website. He asked her what she had in her house, not what new product she could invent, or copy from someone else.

The second point that I'd like to discuss is the notion that Elisha asked her to borrow what she needed (the jars) from her friends and neighbors. This illustrates that getting help where you fall short in your business is biblical. Your support could be a loan or investor, or just simply reaching out or joining a community that can help push you towards success. I've worked with tons of entrepreneurs that are afraid to get help for fear that someone is going to steal their idea. That is one way that the enemy uses to keep you isolated and stuck. Once the widow combined what she had at home, with help from her friends and neighbors she had more than enough to pay all of her debts and to live on. I pray that your oil will never stop flowing.

Father, we humble ourselves and submit to your will and your word. We thank you for all that you are, and we repent for all sins we may have committed both known and unknown.

Lord, I honor you, for I know that it is you that gives all power to be successful in all that I do, for you will fulfill the covenant

of success that you have promised my ancestors. [Deuteronomy 8:18]

Father God, we come to you requesting that you bless every product/service that my business offers including (name product or service that you offer). Lord show me who needs exactly what I'm selling/offering and may they have a pleasant experience.

Lord bless the entire sales processes and allow every aspect of the process to flow easy and pain-free for both myself and my customers.

Lord give me a fresh anointing to create products/services that will resonate with my target audience, and that will increase their quality of life. Lord, show me what services/products aren't working and grant me wisdom to make improvements as needed.

Father thank you for identifying products and services to sell for I am using them to serve others. Lord supply your energy and strength and let everything, every product, and service, bring glory to you, God through Jesus Christ. [1 Peter 4:10-11]

Lord, I dedicate every aspect of my business to you, including my products/services for I know that it is only through you that I am able.

Help me to be diligent and steadfast when selling my products and services. Show me when I need to move and do not allow me to overthink and become stagnant waiting on the perfect moment. Please remove the spirit of perfectionism that may hover over me, for those who wait for the perfect moment will never reap a harvest. [Ecclesiastes 11:4]

Show me the products and services to sell that give you honor for what good does it do to profit and gain the world but to forfeit my soul in the process. [Mark 8:36]

Thank you Lord for identifying my oil, my anointing, may it continue to flow and allow me to provide for my family and for generations to come [2 Kings 4:7] In Jesus name amen.

PRAYER TWENTY SIX: STAFF & EMPLOYEES

Lazy hands make for poverty, but diligent hands bring wealth.
[Proverbs 10:4 NIV]

As your business grows, there will come a time when you will need to hire help. You may already have a few employees, volunteers, or contractors on your team, as they are critical your business success. It's nearly impossible to grow and scale a profitable Kingdom business by yourself, and at some point, you need to solicit the help of others. We built Myavana with the help of volunteers, interns, and contract employees. They did everything from small minute tasks to help us develop our mobile app. Most of the time it was a positive interaction as we gave people an opportunity to help us build from the ground up, and some of our staff went on to create their own successful companies and brands.

It is important that you pray and seek God for every single employee, volunteer, intern, or contractor on your team before you hire them, and continue to cover them daily. Your employees could make or break your company and can cause you much strain and stress if you are not careful and prayerful on who you hire to help build your brand. Although I have several success stories of working with and employing others, I also have stories where we have suffered significant losses at the hands of employees.

Myavana had just gotten funding for our startup and we were excited to expand our team. We had several people working with us on the technical side to free us up to be the face of our company and to expand the vision. My co-founder felt it was a good idea to hire an overseas development firm to help build out the web version of our platform. Our team put together a beautiful working demo and was excited about the full build out.

That summer, we landed our first beauty activation as a hair technology company for Essence Festival in New Orleans. We were super excited as it was the first time we'd made revenue in exchange for goods and services. We decided that we were going to launch our new platform at Essence Festival at the beauty activation. Myavana's success and ability to serve our client was dependent upon on our contractors completing the new website on time.

Long story short, the overseas contractors fell completely short on delivering the website we needed in time for the festival. They did give us a website, but it was nothing like the working demo we put together. To make matters worse, we had given them close to fifteen thousand dollars and had practically nothing to show for it! We were devastated and ended up scrambling to put something together in a few short days, as we had already gotten full payment from our client and spent a good portion of the money in preparation to make the trip.

I truly believe that if we had prayed and asked God for direction concerning working with this development firm, we would have saved thousands of dollars, headache, and frustration. I now make it a priority to pray and await an answer from God for every single person I hire. I don't care if it's for a fifteen dollar project or a fifteen thousand dollar project.

Heavenly Father, I give you all the honor and praise for you are a wonderful and magnificent God. You are worthy, my Lord and God, to receive glory and honor and power, for you created all things, and by your will, they were created and have their being. [Revelation 4:11]

Lord, I ask that you bless every member of my team. Father remove any spirit of fear or timidity and bless them with the power, love, and self-discipline. [2 Timothy 1:7]

Please send me the right staff that will be fruitful with all of

their efforts. May the work of their hands glorify your Kingdom. Your word says that poor is he who works with a negligent hand, but the hand of the diligent makes rich. [Proverbs 10:4]

Allow the fruits of my staff/employee's labor to manifest blessings for my business so that I may sow back into your Kingdom and your perfect will.

Give me the discernment to know without a shadow of a doubt who on my team is working for me and those that are working against me.

Lord, show me how to manage my team and remind me to be just and fair to my employees remembering you, the master of all things is in heaven. [Colossians 4:1]

Thank you, God, for granting me the ability to be a vessel for your children to sow into their lives and their families with the work you have appointed me to do.

Bless every contractor, employee, and volunteer that is on my team, may the blessings, favor, and grace that you have granted me overflow to them. In Jesus name I pray, amen.

PRAYER TWENTY SEVEN: CUSTOMERS

Each of you should use whatever gift you have received to serve others, as faithful stewards of God's grace in its various forms. [1 Peter 4:10 NIV]

There is an age old saying "If you build it, they will come... But that couldn't be further from the truth! It should be renamed, "If you build what they want, they will come. You can find out exactly what the customer wants by using a method I learned from attending startup accelerator programs called customer discovery. Customer discovery is the act of presenting your potential customers with the product or idea before the final product/service is completed while spending the least amount of money possible. I've used variations of the customer discovery method for each business that I have started, and it has proven to be successful every single time. I will share the method with you below.

Don't be afraid to tell people about your product. For some reason, people are scared of sharing their ideas with the mindset that someone is going to "steal" it. It's highly unlikely that they will go through the trouble of re-creating or building your product/brand. Remember, you can't receive feedback if people don't know about it.

Have a basic demo of the product or idea even if it doesn't look appealing or isn't finished. Create what is called in the startup world, an MVP (minimal viable product). An MVP is the most basic version of your product without all the fancy branding or features. An MVP can be a video demo/pitch or a basic platform or application.

Set up a basic website landing page & share it with everyone you know and people you don't know. Your landing page should feature a video of your product demo or pitch. It should also include an email pop up that collects first name, last name, email address, and phone number (optional). This information will be used to obtain feedback from potential customers you won't meet in person. Once you have completed your landing page, share, share, share. Share with people you meet in person, share with your social networks, share with all of your email contacts and create a Facebook ad with your target demographic info to see if you can collect interest from new leads.

Don't be afraid to ask for feedback and set a feedback goal. You may think your idea is magnificent, but you'd be surprised to find out that people might have other suggestions on how to use the product or will suggest product improvement ideas. You will start to notice trends in feedback responses, including product adjustments or improvements. It is essential to set a goal on how much feedback is needed before investing any more money in your product. A good rule of thumb is to aim for a feedback goal of at least fifty people or more.

Determine if your product is a fit for your market & make modifications if needed. You will know based on the feedback if you are on the right track or if it's best to pivot to a different market or make modifications to your idea or product. Obtaining seventy five to eighty percent in overall positive feedback from people you don't know, can provide you with enough information on how to move forward. If you received mixed reviews or less than seventy five percent favorable feedback, it's time to go back to the drawing board and include the input you received to make necessary changes.

Follow up with everyone that provided feedback. If your product is still pre-development, you should send regular email update and include your feedback contact list in your development process. Your customer discovery feedback group will help build a following for your brand and have the potential to become your first customers when you launch.

Lord, I honor you and give you praise. Father, I thank you for birthing in me a plan and a purpose, I thank you for showing

me to whom I am called. I thank you for giving me a group of people to serve and to improve their quality of life through the gifts, talents, and purpose you birthed through me. For Lord, I am your masterpiece. You have created me in Christ Jesus so that I can do the good things that you planned for me long ago. [Ephesians 2:10]

Lord I repent for the misuse or mishandling of any customers in the past whether it be through over commitment, rushed service, poor service, cancelled service, late services, missed deadlines and (name anything that isn't listed). Please forgive me Father and I vow to have the utmost integrity when dealing with customers from this day forward. Therefore, whenever I have an opportunity, I will do good to my customers — especially to those in the family of faith. [Galatians 6:10]

God, I ask that you show me exactly who my customers are. Show me where I can locate them, and how I can best serve them. Give me the tools and resources to identify exactly what my customers need. Show me their pain points and how my products and services are the solutions for their problems. Lord, I will work with enthusiasm, as though I were working for you rather than for people, remembering that you will reward me for the good work that I do. [Ephesians 6:7-8]

Father give me divine insight on the ideal customers and show me what products and services I offer fit best their needs. Lord, I ask that you send me an influx of customers that are in need of what I have to offer, and may their lives be changed for the better. Lord, I ask that every customer I interact with be pleased with my customer service. May there be a positive experience for all that encounter me and that use my products and services.

Lord, I thank you for repeat customers. Father, I thank you for positive customer reviews. Father, I thank you for customers telling their friends and family and converting them to customers. Father, I thank you for the right customers, and I ask that you sever any ties to people that I'm not supposed to serve and replace them with whom you have called me to serve.

I cancel any plan or attack from that adversary that would seek to destroy or sabotage my customer relationships. I break any stronghold or fear associated with finding and seeking out new customers. You Father, have given me a purpose and a gift to share with the world, I will use it well to serve others. [1 Peter 4:10] It is my responsibility to find the people you have for me. Fear will no longer keep me in bondage from promoting my products and services to attract customers to my business. In Jesus name I pray, amen.

PRAYER TWENTY EIGHT: EXPOSURE

In the same way, let your light shine before others, that they may see your good deeds and glorify your Father in heaven. Matthew 5:16 NIV]

One thing I have been particularly good at is garnering media coverage for my businesses. So good that I was even asked to contribute two nationally recognized media platforms. People have often inquired me how I was able to land media features and how they can utilize media and press for their business. The high-level answer is simple - create a brand story that resonates with your target audience, don't be afraid to share your story, and believe that you and your brand is newsworthy.

How many times have you bought into a brand just because you liked what they represented? If you are faced with two products that perform about the same, you are going to go with the brand that has a story that aligns with who you are and what you represent. For example, what's the difference between Target and Walmart? They both sell the same items, yet cater to different audiences. This is also true for your business when you tell your brand story; you give people the option to decide if they want to support you. Your brand story is what sets you apart from other brands, and will build a tribe of supporters.

Next, you must be willing to share your story and talk about your business. If no one knows about what you are selling and what you have to offer, they won't be able to support you. One of the most popular ways to share your business is on social media. You can do this via paid social media advertising and by sharing your business on your personal and business profiles. I highly recommend investing in paid social media advertising as it can guarantee to showcase your brand in front of your specific target audience. You can also pitch yourself for media and press by identifying media outlets that cater to your audience and submit your story.

You can gain more exposure by seeking out speaking engagements at conferences and seminars that are looking for experts in your industry. Pitch for speaking engagements by searching event websites and social media and submit your story highlighting your brand expertise. The more people you get in front of, the more people will associate you as an expert, and as the go-to product or person to meet their needs. Consider creating an eBook or other expert-driven products, if you have an eBook or training featuring your expertise, it already separates you from other brands and paints a picture that you are the authority. Who wouldn't want to purchase from and connect with an expert when choosing what product or service they are going to support.

Finally, you have to believe that you are worthy and valuable. I've had to overcome issues in this area. At one point, I believed the lies that the enemy would whisper to me telling me that what I had to offer wasn't good enough to share. I would be hesitant to share my brand for fear of what others thought. One night, God spoke to me in a dream and said "Let your light shine [Matthew 5:16] by walking in your purpose [Ephesians 2:10] as a result you will love yourself, and love others [Matthew 22:39].

Father God, I honor you, love you, and thank you for loving me, caring for me, and always thinking of me. I thank you, Lord, for your perfect timing and for creating me for such a time as this. Your love fills me up when I am empty and lifts me up when I am down. I give you all the praise, all the honor, and I worship you. I thank you for giving my business the exposure it needs to reach the people you have called me to serve.

Lord, I repent for coveting the exposure and success of others. I ask that you forgive me for letting fear get in the way of promoting the business you gave me. You have permitted me to let my light shine so that others may see your good deeds and glorify you. [Matthew 5:16] No longer will I feel unworthy to share my gifts and business with others.

Father, you have given me wisdom so that my business will shine brightly in the sky. My business is my ministry, and my righteous living will bring others to Christ and allow my business to shine continuously, bright like the stars. [Daniel 12:3]

My business deserves to be seen by others. I am confident in my abilities and the ability to handle all exposure that you bring my way. I can be confident of all this because of my great trust in you God, through Christ. It is not that I think I am qualified to do anything on my own, for my qualification comes from you, God. [2 Corinthians 3:4-5]

I cancel any attempt of my adversaries that would seek to block, pervert, or destroy the platforms in which you have given me to promote my business. I speak blessings over every single future and current advertising, media, and exposure campaigns that I have in place for my business.

I decree and declare supranational exposure opportunities and platforms will be created for my brand and me. Media coverage and news articles, sold out events, speaking engagements, and strategies for viral campaigns are released to me now. I will proclaim that it was you God who awarded me these opportunities and not myself, for I am humble and give you all the praise. In Jesus name, I pray, amen.

PRAYER TWENTY NINE: INTEGRITY

And you yourself must be an example to them by doing good works of every kind. Let everything you do reflect the integrity and seriousness of your teaching. [Titus 2:7 NLT]

Integrity is a big deal that most people take for granted in business. As a business owner, I work hard to treat other companies the way I'd like mine to be treated. [Luke 6:31] If I don't want anyone to steal from me I don't steal from them. If I don't want to be lied to, I don't lie. If I want to be treated fairly, I make sure to treat others fairly. Some of you won't get far in business just because you are not operating with integrity.

We forget that when we watch pirated films and shows and illegally download software and music that we are stealing. How would you feel if someone illegally downloaded a copy of your eBook, or took your products directly from you? Not good right? How many times have you given the enemy a foothold to come on in and wreak havoc in your business, because of your lack of integrity?

By now I am sure you are familiar with the Bible verse:

Do not be deceived: God cannot be mocked. A man reaps what he sows. [Galatians 6:7 NIV]

How is it that we can ask and plead with God to bless us in our businesses when we lie, steal, and cheat from others? How can we expect people to pay their invoices for services when we are dodging bill collectors and making late payments?

God wants to bless you and your business beyond your wildest dreams, but if you are not living a righteous and integrity-filled life, you only have limited access to his blessings. When you are living with integrity, your entire generation will be blessed for the word says their children will be mighty in the land; the generation of the upright will be blessed. [Psalm 112:2] If you haven't been operating and living an integrity-filled life, all is not lost. Jesus Christ died on the cross for our sins so that we can repent and be freed!

Here are a few ways in which you can live and operate your business with integrity:

- Treat others the way you want to be treated
- Pay your bills on time and pay what you owe
- Do not use illegally downloadable software and tools for your home or your business
- Don't bad mouth other businesses or business owners - better yet, mind your business
- Report your correct amount of earnings on your taxes and don't try to lie to the IRS because you don't want to pay
- Never lie or lower your income so that you can receive benefits that you don't qualify for
- Be transparent
- Stop over promising and under delivering
- Only put out your best work
- Respect your customers and listen to their concerns
- Do unto to others as you would have them to do you
- Follow through on your word

Lord, I give thanks to you, for you are good! Your faithful love endures forever. [1 Chronicles 16:34] Father I enter your gates with thanksgiving; I go into your courts with praise.

I Give thanks to you and praise your name. [Psalm 100:4]

Thank you, Lord, for sending your son Jesus to wipe away my sins so that I can live a life of righteousness and holiness. I vow to operate my business with integrity. Because of my integrity, you will uphold me and set me in your presence forever. [Psalm 41:12]

Lord, I repent for not always living and operating my business in integrity. I repent for using pirated software, streaming pirated movies and television shows, not following or delivering on services or products as promised, stealing from other business owners, gossiping about other business owners, not being transparent, lying to customers, overpromising and under delivering, overextending myself and (name anything that isn't listed). For your word declares that whoever walks in integrity walks securely, but whoever takes crooked paths will be found out. [Proverbs 10:9]

If there is an area in my life or business in which I lack integrity, please reveal it to me. For I know that as a child of God I must walk in integrity so that my children and my generation will be blessed. [Proverbs 20:7]

I am careful to be honorable before you Lord, but I also want everyone else to see that I am honorable. [2 Corinthians 8:21]

My business will stand on principles that are true, and honorable, and right, and pure, and lovely, and admirable, and things that are excellent and worthy of praise. [Philippians 4:8]

In everything I do, I will set an example by doing what is good and showing them integrity. [Titus 2:7]

I will not merely just listen to the word on how to live and operate a business with integrity, and so deceive myself. I will do what it says. For anyone who listens to the word but does not do what it says is like someone who looks at his face in a mirror and, after looking at himself, goes away and immediately forgets what he looks like. But whoever looks intently into the perfect law that gives freedom, and continues in it—not forgetting what they have heard, but doing it—they will be blessed in what they do. [James 1:22-25] In Jesus name I pray, amen.

PRAYER THIRTY: FINANCES

A good person leaves an inheritance for their children's children, but a sinner's wealth is stored up for the righteous. [Proverbs 13:22 NIV]

Money is the answer to everything! [Ecclesiastes 10:9] It is the resource in which you can accomplish all things. You need money to build, grow, and maintain your life and business. God uses money in the natural to help manifest things that are already in place in the supernatural. He uses your tithes, offerings, and money that you sow into others to accomplish his good works, and this is why the enemy attacks the finances of believers. The enemy knows that if the righteous are wealthy, then they will be the answer to the world's problems. Living in financial abundance isn't just for special people or for those that are born rich. You too can be prosperous in your business and your finances. Here are four steps to achieving biblical financial success.

Break all curses that are blocking your generational blessings. Generational curses can and will stop you from ever amassing true riches. If your bloodline is cursed the enemy has a legal right to block you from receiving your generational blessings. Your generational blessings are the resources, money, favor, and grace, which are attached to your bloodline. It's your inheritance that is waiting for you in the heavens. You must repent for all sins you have committed and the sins of your past generations. You have the power and authority by the blood of Jesus Christ to intercede for your family and generations to come. For the Bible says "Their children will be successful everywhere; an entire generation of godly people will be blessed. They themselves will be wealthy, and their good deeds will last forever". [Psalm 112:2-3 NLT]

Get delivered from having a poverty mentality. When you struggle with this mindset, you will operate your businesses and your finances from a place of lack. You believe that God's resources are limited and will run out. You may also be terrified of investing money on yourself and for your business. You often quit projects before they even start because you don't know or believe that God can send you what you need. You are afraid to do things that "everyone else is doing." You think that there are not enough customers, money, and resources to do what God has called you to do. God created all the heavens and the earth, so he can surely supply your every need, especially if you are in alignment with his will for your life. For the Bible declares:

Keep on asking, and you will receive what you ask for. Keep on seeking, and you will find. Keep on knocking, and the door will be opened to you. For everyone who asks, receives. Everyone who seeks finds. And to everyone who knocks, the door will be opened. [Matthew 7:7-8 NLT]

Check yourself and make sure you are serving God and not the Spirit of Mammon.

No one can serve two masters; for either he will hate the one and love the other, or he will be devoted to the one and despise the other. You cannot serve God and mammon. [Matthew 6:24 AMP]

Where and how you spend your money dictates which master you serve. You can serve and honor God by tithing and sowing back into his Kingdom. If you want to see an open heaven, commit to tithing and sowing into your church, a ministry, and others following the will of God. This is explained in Malachi chapter three:

Will a mere mortal rob God? Yet you rob me. "But you ask, 'How are we robbing you?' "In tithes and offerings. You are under a curse—your whole nation—because you are robbing me. Bring the whole tithe into the storehouse, that there may be food in my house. Test me in this," says the Lord Almighty, "and see if I will not throw open the floodgates of heaven and pour out so much blessing that there will not be room enough to store it. [Malachi 3:8-10

NLT]

You must adequately manage the money and resources God has given you. You can no longer live day to day, month to month, or even year to year. Your financial plan should include managing and creating wealth for your children's children. How do you do this if you are in debt or living paycheck to paycheck? By saving money, even if it's as little as ten dollars per paycheck. For the Bible says –

Dishonest money dwindles away, but whoever gathers money little by little makes it grow. [Proverbs 13:11 NIV]

Pay God first (sow into his Kingdom), pay yourself next (save), then pay your debts, bills, and living expenses. God can and will supply your every need, but you will have to put in the work. You may need to make adjustments including cutting back on your spending, getting a part-time job, going back to work full-time, selling additional products, or taking on consulting work and becoming a freelancer. You also must be accountable for every penny that is spent in your business and personal life, because so many people have no idea where their money is going. You can not be lazy when managing your money; it is an active, not passive process. For the Bible states:

So if you have not been trustworthy in handling worldly wealth, who will trust you with true riches? [Luke 16:11 NIV]

I praise you Lord for your great love and for the wonderful things you have done for me and my business. For you satisfy me when I am thirsty, and you fill my hunger with good things. [Psalm 107:8-9] I give a joyful thanks to you Father, you have qualified me to share in the inheritance of your holy people in the kingdom of light. [Colossians 1:13]

Lord, I repent for not surrendering my finances entirely over to you. I repent for trying to do everything in my own strength and for not leaning on you for direction. I also repent for not tithing and sowing as I should. Father, I thank you for being the Lord of my finances. I commit to serving you, and you only. By the authority granted to me through the blood of Jesus Christ, I

cast out the spirit of mammon in me, who has no legal right to rule over my business and my finances. I send you mammon and your co-conspirators into the abyss.

Father give me direction on ways that I can grow and maintain my business so that I may leave an inheritance for my children's children. Father, release to me the sinner's wealth that is stored up for the righteous [Proverbs 13:22] Show me how to be a good steward over my finances so that you will trust me with true riches. [Luke 16:11]

Lord, please send rain at the proper time from your rich treasury in the heavens and bless all the work that I do. For I will lend to many nations, but I will never need to borrow from them. [Deuteronomy 28:12] In Jesus name, I pray, amen.

PRAYER THIRTY ONE:
FOCUS

Look straight ahead, and fix your eyes on what lies before you.
[Proverbs 4:25 NLT]

As small business owners, entrepreneurs, and creatives it's easy to lose focus and become distracted with what God has called you to do. If you are anything like me, you are bursting with ideas, businesses, and ventures. I have particularly struggled in this area as I was diagnosed years ago with ADHD. I would experience issues with focusing on tasks or I would hyper focus on projects, and often they would be things that weren't going to bear any fruit. I battled with staying focused on the big picture, and I enjoyed working on quick projects that would give me an immediate result.

Eventually, I would hit a brick wall when something didn't work out how I wanted it to work, and when I wanted it to work. I would become distracted ignoring the grand scheme of it all and begin to do meaningless busy work just because I was bored. I had to learn that there is a process to everything, sometimes yielding immediate results and sometimes the reward is further down the line. I needed to learn how to stay committed and focused on God's promises even when I didn't know or understand how I was going to get there. I had to stay focused even when working on tasks or projects connected to my purpose that I didn't like. I had to quit using ADHD as an excuse to dip out of things early because I had lost interest. I had to be delivered and healed from distraction.

I am sure we all have experienced seasons where our focus was off. We were searching for the quick fix to our problems without first consulting God to see if we are even on the right path. You must search your heart and check your motives for everything that you are doing. Ask yourself, have I committed everything to seeing this vision through? Am I working on the vision that God has purposed me? Am I only working to keep up with appearances or to satisfy my flesh? Am I being intentional about seeking God for all things?

We all know that person where every week they are in a new network marketing business. They start out selling makeup, then are selling teas, next month they are trying to sign you up to sell life insurance. Now there is nothing wrong with direct sales businesses, but with the low startup costs, you get tons of people who are looking for a quick fix and haven't sat with God for direction as it pertains their purpose.

The enemy uses the spirit of distraction to abort your purpose. Satan recognizes that if you are not focused on the promises and plans that God has for you, then it will be easy for you to give up prematurely. Your adversary will often dangle many different enticing fruits in front of you, fill your mind with negative self-talk, and cause disorder in your family and personal life to keep you from fulfilling your purpose. Know that to receive the blessings of God you must remain steadfast and focused. I hope that after praying over your business, you realize that:

- You need to be focused and intentional when you pray for your business
- You need to be focused in on God's plan if you want heaven's backing
- When you are focused and walking in purpose everything you need will be given to you
- There are unlimited resources, so you don't need to focus in on what God is doing for others

Father God, I love you, and I thank you. Everything you have created is good, and I will not reject any of it, but receive it with thanks. For I know it is made acceptable by your word God and through prayer. [1 Timothy 4:4-5]

Father, I repent for not staying focused and committed to tasks. I repent for working only on things that satisfy my will, and not submitting to your will.

Because you, sovereign Lord is guiding me in my business, I will not be disgraced. Therefore, I have set my face like a stone, determined to do your will. And I know that I will not be put to shame. [Isaiah 50:7]

Father, I am focused, and I commit everything I do for my business to you Lord, and for that, my plans will succeed. [Proverbs 16:3]

Lord, I will not copy the behavior and customs of this world. I ask that you, God, will transform me into a new person by changing the way I think. So that I will learn to know your will for me, which is good and pleasing and perfect. [Romans 12:2]

Father, I am staying focused looking only straight ahead, and fixing my eyes on what lies before me and not what others are doing. [Proverbs 4:25] I will think about the things of heaven, not the things of earth. [Colossians 3:2]

Father, I am seeking your Kingdom above all else and living righteously, and I ask that you give me everything I need to succeed in my business. [Matthew 6:33]

Father, you say in your word, "I will guide you along the best pathway for your life. I will advise you and watch over you." [Psalm 32:8] Don't be afraid, for I am with you. Don't be discouraged, for I am your God. I will strengthen you and help you. I will hold you up with my victorious right hand. [Isaiah 41:10]" In Jesus name, I pray, amen.

THANK YOU!

Thank you for completing **31 Prayers for Spiritual Wealth**. May the floodgates of spiritual wealth be released to you in the name of Jesus. May you be healed and delivered from every stronghold and attack of the enemy for he was defeated over two thousand years ago. I pray that you realized that you have an inheritance and that it is has been released to you. We are in an open heaven season so continue to seek the Kingdom of God, and all things you need will be added unto you. [Matthew 6:33] To learn more about spiritual wealth visit visit www.chanelemartin.com.

ABOUT THE AUTHOR

Chanel E'bone Martin, a Chemical Engineer by trade and a Kingdom entrepreneur by calling. A prophetic business voice, technology company founder, serial entrepreneur, and founder of Blessed Profits, Chanel has cracked the code on how to successfully brand, fund, and launch small businesses. Having raised nearly a half million in funding and completing two successful crowdfunding campaigns, Chanel has created eBooks, webinars, and workbooks to help small business owners get the funding they need.

In addition to teaching small business owners her fundraising secrets, Chanel also coaches brands on how to maximize their brand's exposure. Chanel and her companies have been featured in national publications and broadcasts including The Real, BET, Black Enterprise, Essence, Ebony, Forbes, Yahoo, Business Insider, and more. As wife and mom of two, Chanel lives by the mantra "walk in your purpose and let your light shine". You can learn more about Chanel by visiting her website www.chanelemartin.com.

Made in the USA
Monee, IL
01 July 2022

98929680R10069